Greek and Roman Mythology

Titles in the World History Series

**WORLD
HISTORY SERIES** ■ ■ ■

Greek and Roman Mythology

by
Don Nardo

Lucent Bool 3 1901 02682 4542 , CA 92198-9011

Library of Congress Cataloging-in-Publication Data

Nardo, Don, 1947–
    Greek and Roman mythology / by Don Nardo.
        p. cm. — (World history series)
    Includes bibliographical references and index.
    Summary: Examines the historical development of Greco-
Roman mythology, its heroes, and its influence on the history
of Western civilization.
    ISBN 1-56006-308-4 (alk. paper)
    1. Mythology, Classical—Juvenile literature. [1. Mythology,
Classical.] I. Title. II. Series.
BL725.N37   1998
292.1'3—dc21   97–7481
                                                           CIP
                                                            AC

Copyright 1998 by Lucent Books, Inc., P.O. Box 289011,
San Diego, California 92198-9011

Printed in the U.S.A.

Contents

Foreword

Each year on the first day of school, nearly every history teacher faces the task of explaining why his or her students should study history. One logical answer to this question is that exploring what happened in our past explains how the things we often take for granted—our customs, ideas, and institutions—came to be. As statesman and historian Winston Churchill put it, "Every nation or group of nations has its own tale to tell. Knowledge of the trials and struggles is necessary to all who would comprehend the problems, perils, challenges, and opportunities which confront us today." Thus, a study of history puts modern ideas and institutions in perspective. For example, though the founders of the United States were talented and creative thinkers, they clearly did not invent the concept of democracy. Instead, they adapted some democratic ideas that had originated in ancient Greece and with which the Romans, the British, and others had experimented. An exploration of these cultures, then, reveals their very real connection to us through institutions that continue to shape our daily lives.

Another reason often given for studying history is the idea that lessons exist in the past from which contemporary societies can benefit and learn. This idea, although controversial, has always been an intriguing one for historians. Those who agree that society can benefit from the past often quote philosopher George Santayana's famous statement, "Those who cannot remember the past are condemned to repeat it." Historians who ascribe to Santayana's philosophy believe that, for example, studying the events that led up to the major world wars or other significant historical events would allow society to chart a different and more favorable course in the future.

Just as difficult as convincing students to realize the importance of studying history is the search for useful and interesting supplementary materials that present historical events in a context that can be easily understood. The volumes in Lucent Books' World History Series attempt to present a broad, balanced, and penetrating view of the march of history. Ancient Egypt's important wars and rulers, for example, are presented against the rich and colorful backdrop of Egyptian religious, social, and cultural developments. The series engages the reader by enhancing historical events with these cultural contexts. For example, in *Ancient Greece*, the text covers the role of women in that society. Slavery is discussed in *The Roman Empire*, as well as how slaves earned their freedom. The numerous and varied aspects of everyday life in these and other societies are explored in each volume of the series. Additionally, the series covers the major political, cultural, and philosophical ideas as the torch of civilization is passed from ancient Mesopotamia and Egypt, through Greece, Rome, Medieval Europe, and other world cultures, to the modern day.

The material in the series is formatted in a thorough, precise, and organized manner. Each volume offers the reader a comprehensive and clearly written overview of an important historical event or period. The topic under discussion is placed in a broad historical context. For example, *The Italian Renaissance* begins with a discussion of the High Middle Ages and the loss of central control that allowed certain Italian cities to develop artistically. The book ends by looking forward to the Reformation and interpreting the societal changes that grew out of the Renaissance. Thus, students are not only involved in an historical era, but also enveloped by the events leading up to that era and the events following it.

One important and unique feature in the World History Series is the primary and secondary source quotations that richly supplement each volume. These quotes are useful in a number of ways. First, they allow students access to sources they would not normally be exposed to because of the difficulty and obscurity of the original source. The quotations range from interesting anecdotes to farsighted cultural perspectives and are drawn from historical witnesses both past and present. Second, the quotes demonstrate how and where historians themselves derive their information on the past as they strive to reach a consensus on historical events. Lastly, all of the quotes are footnoted, familiarizing students with the citation process and allowing them to verify quotes and/or look up the original source if the quote piques their interest.

Finally, the books in the World History Series provide a detailed launching point for further research. Each book contains a bibliography specifically geared toward student research. A second, annotated bibliography introduces students to all the sources the author consulted when compiling the book. A chronology of important dates gives students an overview, at a glance, of the topic covered. Where applicable, a glossary of terms is included.

In short, the series is designed not only to acquaint readers with the basics of history, but also to make them aware that their lives are a part of an ongoing human saga. Perhaps they will then come to the same realization as famed historian Arnold Toynbee. In his monumental work, *A Study of History*, he wrote about becoming aware of history flowing through him in a mighty current, and of his own life "welling like a wave in the flow of this vast tide."

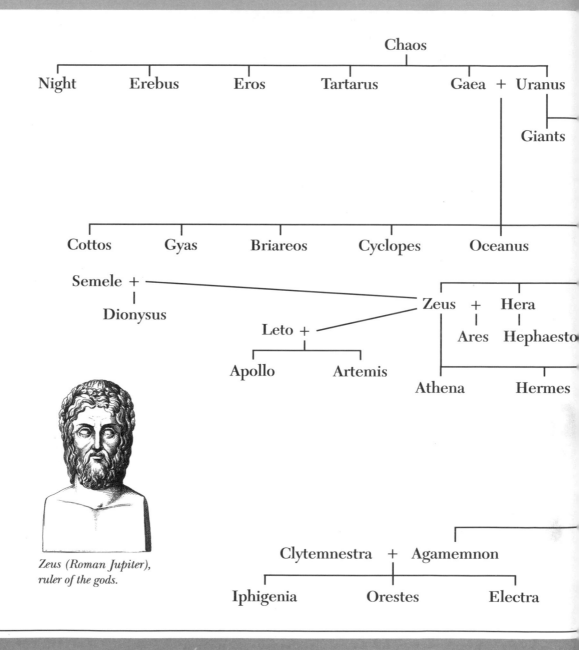

Zeus (Roman Jupiter), ruler of the gods.

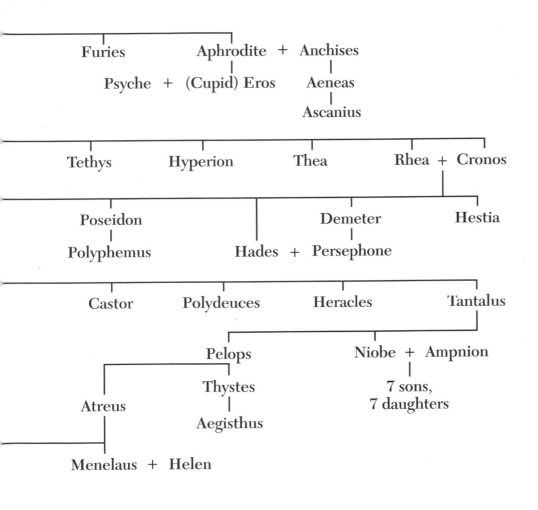

Furies   Aphrodite + Anchises

Psyche + (Cupid) Eros   Aeneas

Ascanius

Tethys   Hyperion   Thea   Rhea + Cronos

Poseidon   Demeter   Hestia

Polyphemus   Hades + Persephone

Castor   Polydeuces   Heracles   Tantalus

Pelops   Niobe + Ampnion

Thystes   7 sons,
7 daughters

Atreus   Aegisthus

Menelaus + Helen

Timeless Tales of Gods and Humans

For more than a thousand years the Mediterranean world was dominated, both politically and culturally, by the Greeks and the Romans. The merging of many elements of the two cultures—exemplified by widespread Roman adaptation of the Greeks' supremely elegant and rational art, architecture, and literature—is often referred to as classical civilization. One of the most important and far-reaching products of classical culture was a rich legacy of Greco-Roman myths, the stories, characters, and moral lessons of which profoundly influenced the art and literature of later societies, including our own.

What Constitutes Myth?

To better understand and appreciate the classic Greek and Roman myths, one needs first to consider what these myths were and where they came from. The English word *myth* derives from the Greek word *muthos*, meaning a spoken or written story, and the ancient Greeks defined the word *muthologia*, or mythology, as talking about or retelling stories. It is immediately apparent that this definition for myths is very vague and general. In fact, no precise definition exists and the stories included in various mythology collections, includ-ing this one, are of many types. Some are folktales. These are usually fanciful stories that were originally aimed at uneducated residents of rural farming communities and intended either as pure entertainment or to teach a moral lesson. The main characters of folktales are most commonly ordinary men and women or animals. Examples range from fables in which animals can talk to stories in which ordinary humans find themselves thrust into extraordinary circumstances, such as the tale of Baucis and Philemon, about two aging peasants who unwittingly welcome the god Zeus into their home.

Another kind of myth is the saga or legend. Like folktales, such stories often feature fantastic, mystical, and/or superhuman elements and characters, such as confrontations between people and gods or monsters. Unlike folktales, however, sagas are based on actual characters and events, the memories of which have become dimmed and distorted by the passage of time. The famous *Iliad*, the epic story of a phase of the Trojan War, now known to be a real event, is an example of this type of myth. The tales of Agamemnon, one of the heroes of that war, and the murderous events that later rocked his family and royal house constitute another example of mythical saga.

The Greek gods assemble atop Mount Olympus. Zeus, "the cloud-gatherer," sits on his throne with his wife, Hera, by his right side.

Scholars often refer to a third variety of myth as pure or true myth. Included in this group are stories relating directly to the origins and development of religion and ritual. Some of the works of the seventh-century B.C. Greek poet Hesiod are examples. His *Theogony*, for instance, which chronicles the creation of the gods and humans, provides a view of the relationship between mortals and immortals that became standard in Greek religious worship.

One thing that all of these kinds of myths have in common is that they frequently deal with the gods and their interactions with human beings, and some experts see in this commonality a loose but workable definition for myths. For example, in their highly esteemed book, *Classical Mythology*, scholars Mark Morford and Robert Lenardon state: "*Myth* is a comprehensive (but not exclusive) term for stories primarily concerned with the gods and man's relationship with them."[1]

This preoccupation with stories about gods and humans is common to the mythologies of all ancient peoples. What made the Greeks different (and also in large degree the Romans, who based much of their own mythology on that of the Greeks) was that they pictured their gods as having human form and even human emotions. These human characteristics made these divinely mysterious beings seem more rational, comprehensible, and, in terms of worship, more easily approachable. As famed classical scholar Edith Hamilton puts it:

> The Greeks made their gods in their own image. That had not entered the mind of man before. Until then, gods had had no semblance of reality. They were unlike all living things. In Egypt, a towering colossus, immobile, beyond the power of the imagination to endow with movement . . . or a rigid figure, a woman with a cat's head suggesting inflexible human cruelty. Or a monstrous mysterious sphinx, aloof from all that lives. In Mesopotamia, bas-reliefs of bestial shapes unlike any beast ever known, men with birds' heads and lions with bulls' heads . . . creations of artists who were intent on producing something never seen except in their own minds, the very consummation of unreality. These and their like were what the pre-Greek world worshipped. One need only place beside them in imagination any Greek statue of a god, so normal and natural with all its beauty, to perceive what a new idea had come into the world. With its coming, the universe became rational.[2]

The Age of Heroes

In retrospect, that the heroes and gods of the Greek myths were so human or humanlike is not surprising, for we now know that a large number of these stories were based on real people and events of an era long predating the so-called golden age of the classical Greeks. That classic age—in which city-states, most notably Athens, produced democratic ideals and great art, architecture, and literature—approximately encompassed the sixth through the fourth centuries B.C. But many centuries before this splendid society of Pericles, Socrates, Plato, and the imposing Parthenon temple, Greece and the Aegean island sphere had been the home of a more archaic, yet in many ways no less impressive, civilization.

That civilization, in what historians now call the Heroic Age (also the Bronze Age because people used weapons and tools made of bronze), consisted largely of two groups of early Greeks. As early as 2000 B.C. a culturally advanced people now called the Minoans (after Minos, a legendary king of the island of Crete) built magnificent island palaces and with their huge fleets of cargo vessels and warships dominated the region. For a long time they held sway over the less-advanced and perhaps more warlike Mycenaeans, who lived primarily on the Greek mainland. Vague memories of the interactions of these two cultures survived the centuries in the form of myths like that of Theseus, in which a mainland hero rescues hostages condemned to be eaten by a monster, half man and half bull, on Crete.

Eventually, Minoan power declined and by about 1400 B.C. the Mycenaeans, having become masters of the Aegean, were raiding the coasts of neighboring regions. Memories of these exploits would later give rise to some of the most important of all Greek myths. Scholars now believe that the military expedition against Troy depicted in the *Iliad* was led by Mycenaean warlords, probably including some bearing the names of Agamemnon, Ajax, Odysseus, and other figures identified in the epic poem as Greek kings.

About 1100 B.C. Mycenaean power, already in decline, collapsed as the Aegean sphere underwent invasion and catastrophic social and cultural upheaval. The three to four centuries that followed constituted a "dark age" about which little is known, but it is fairly certain that these years, characterized by widespread poverty, illiteracy, and despair, marked Greek civilization's lowest ebb. During this period memories of the leaders and events of the bygone age of heroes slowly crystallized into widely popular myths. According to historian Peter Connolly, for centuries these stories "were handed down verbally from generation to generation through the bards [wandering poets]. Each bard would add his own color to the story placing increasing emphasis on the characters, often replacing fact with fantasy."[3] By the eighth century B.C., when a more prosperous Greece was emerging from the dark age, Homer and other legendary bards routinely recited these tales, some of them, like the *Iliad*, thousands of lines long.

This sixteenth-century engraving is the artist's conception of the Greek poet Homer, of whom no authentic portraits or busts have survived.

The Sources for Myths

Homer and the other bards, therefore, were the earliest important sources for the Greek myths. Hesiod, who wrote his *Theogony* and *Works and Days* perhaps a century after Homer, was another primary source, especially for creation myths. Other important Greek sources include the *Homeric Hymns*, composed by a number of unknown writers between the eighth and fourth centuries B.C.; the odes of the great lyric poet Pindar, who began writing toward the end of the sixth century B.C.; the plays of the renowned fifth-century B.C. Athenian dramatists Aeschylus, Sophocles, Euripides, and Aristophanes, many of which have mythological themes, especially relating to the sagas of the early Greek royal houses; Herodotus, now known as the "father of history," whose fifth-century B.C. work on the Greek and Persian wars contains many references to local myths; Apollonius of Rhodes and other poets who lived and worked in Alexandria, Egypt, in the mid-third century B.C.; and Lucian, a satirist who wrote in the second century A.D. All of these writers were inspired by very old tales of the Greek gods and the humans with whom they interacted.

By contrast, the major Roman myth tellers had two main sources of inspiration. When Rome's increasingly powerful empire absorbed the Greek states of the eastern Mediterranean in the last two centuries B.C., the Romans, who greatly admired Greek culture, eagerly absorbed many of the popular Greek myths. Making the transition an easy one was the fact that a number of the Roman gods by that time had become Romanized versions of Greek deities (for instance, the Roman Minerva had become the equivalent of Athena, Greek goddess of war and wisdom). The most prolific Roman reteller of the Greek myths was the first-century B.C. poet Ovid, who presented detailed versions of most of the popular myths in his *Metamorphoses*.

The other major inspiration for Roman mythology was early Roman history. Latin writers of Ovid's time, particularly Virgil in his epic poem the *Aeneid* and Livy in his famous history of Rome, glorified the city's founding fathers and their deeds in an epic manner. These stories, unlike most Greek myths, only rarely depicted the gods getting involved in human endeavors. Instead, they often immortalized military and political heroes and members of illustrious Roman families, in the process commenting on and attempting to perpetuate traditional moral values. Thus Roman writers managed to press a stamp of Roman individuality on what we now call classical mythology at the same time that they embellished and passed on the traditional Greek myths that had captured their imaginations. It is not difficult to see why the Romans were so fascinated; in volumes like this one and those listed in its bibliographies, readers continue to revel in these charming, timeless tales of gods and humans.

Chapter

1 Fire from Heaven: The Creation of the Gods and Humans

"Hail, daughters of Zeus!" wrote Hesiod in his *Theogony*. "Give me sweet song, to celebrate the holy race of gods who live forever."[4] The daughters of Zeus, leader of the gods, were the nine Muses, born of the goddess Mnemosyne (Memory) at the foot of the sacred Mount Olympus, home of the gods. The Greeks believed that a person's talent at singing, acting, writing poetry, or other artistic endeavors was a gift endowed by the Muses; and Hesiod was convinced that these deities had given him the gift of "sweet song" one day while he was tending his sheep. It is not surprising, therefore, that in preparing to tell how all things came to be, he called upon the divine Muses to inspire him:

> Tell how the gods and earth arose at first, and rivers and the boundless swollen sea and shining stars, and the broad heaven above, and how the gods divided up their wealth and how they shared their honors, how they first captured Olympus with its many folds. Tell me these things, Olympian Muses, tell from the beginning, which first came to be?[5]

Hesiod then launched into the story of the creation, a tale that was later enriched by the playwrights Aristophanes and Aeschylus and other writers.

An ancient Roman statue, now in Rome's Vatican Museum, depicts Hesiod, the seventh-century B.C. poet.

The Earth and Earliest Gods Emerge

In the beginning, uncounted ages ago, there was only a great hollow void in which the seeds and basic elements of all things swirled randomly together in a shapeless mass. This void was called Chaos. After a very long time—just how long no god or human can say—Chaos gave birth to two children, Night and Erebus, the latter being the dark, still depths where death resides. Both Night and Erebus were black, silent, and endless.

More long ages passed; then suddenly, and in some mysterious way that no one can explain, from the terrifying blackness of Night and Erebus sprang Eros, or Love. Some say that Eros may have hatched from an egg. According to Aristophanes in his play *Birds*, for example:

> Then Night . . . brought forth in her nest within Erebus's breast an Egg . . . from whence was born, as the months rolled on, great Eros, the ever desired, with wings on his shoulders of shining gold, as swift in the storm in his flying. . . . No gods were above us until turbulent Love had affected a cosmic communion.[6]

Indeed, Eros made all communion, or the coming together of things, possible. He brought light to pierce the darkness, and through his influence, order began to appear in the void. The heavier elements slowly settled out and became the earth, and the lighter parts drifted upward and became the sky. Far under the earth, a dark region called Tartarus remained. But above the earth, in the heavens, the sun, moon, and stars appeared; and on the earth itself, the land and sea became separate, rivers flowed to the sea, and trees and plants grew and multiplied across the face of the land. The earth was endowed with the personality of Gaea, Mother Earth, and the heavens personified the spirit of Uranus, Father Heaven.

Gaea and Uranus had many children, the first beings recognizable as living creatures. But these were quite unlike any creatures now known. As Edith Hamilton explains:

> Just as we believe that the earth was once inhabited by strange gigantic creatures, so did the Greeks. They did not, however, think of them as huge lizards and mammoths, but as somewhat like men and yet unhuman. They had the shattering, overwhelming strength of earthquake and hurricane and volcano. In the tales about them they do not seem really alive, but rather to belong to a world where as yet there was no life, only tremendous movements of irresistible forces lifting up the mountains and scooping out the seas.[7]

The first three of the brood were horrifying monsters, each possessing fifty heads and a hundred hands. Their names were Cottos, Gyas, and Briareos. Next came three huge and powerful creatures, each bearing a single eye in the middle of its forehead, who became known as the Cyclopes, which means "wheel eyed."

Finally, Gaea and Uranus produced the twelve Titans, who looked similar to humans but who were much larger and stronger. Among the Titans were Oceanus and Tethys, who took charge of the sea; Hyperion and Thea, deities of the sun and moon, respectively; Rhea, who would later come to be called the "Great Mother"; and

Cronos (whom the Romans called Saturn), the youngest and most powerful of all.

Like nearly all mothers, Gaea loved all of her children, no matter how ugly; but Uranus hated his children, especially the six extremely ugly monsters. So he swept them up and hid them in secret dark places beneath the earth's surface. This behavior distressed Gaea greatly, and she conspired with Cronos and the other Titans to stage a rebellion against Uranus. In the ensuing fight, Cronos wounded his father and drops of his blood showered down. The drops that landed in the sea gave birth to Aphrodite (the Roman Venus), goddess of love, and the drops that touched the earth spawned two races of fearsome creatures—the Giants, primitive beings who wore animal skins, and the serpent-haired Furies, who would later become the merciless tormentors of humans who shed blood. The bleeding Uranus finally lost the battle and Cronos imprisoned him in the shadowy regions of Tartarus, the underworld.

Battle for the Universe

Now that Uranus was out of the way, mighty Cronos assumed the kingship of heaven and married his fellow Titan Rhea. They began to have children of their own, but Cronos feared that his offspring might rebel against him just as he had rebelled against Uranus. So, as soon as each child was born, Cronos swallowed it whole, storing it deep within his gigantic body. This ritual occurred five times in a row and finally poor Rhea, despairing over the loss of so many children, determined to put an end to her husband's grisly practice. When

Rhea gave birth to her sixth child, Zeus (the Roman Jupiter or Jove), she hid the baby in a cave on the island of Crete. She knew that Cronos would expect her to hand over a child for him to devour, of course, but she also knew that he was somewhat dull witted and would therefore be easy to hoodwink. According to Hesiod:

> To the great lord, the son of Heaven, the past king of the gods [Cronos], she handed, solemnly, all wrapped in swaddling-clothes, a giant stone. He seized it in his hands and thrust it down into his belly, fool! He did not know his son, no stone, was left behind, unhurt and undefeated.[8]

But in her ruse, Rhea had unwittingly set in motion a momentous series of events. Zeus's preservation and safekeeping in Crete set the stage for the downfall of the Titans and rise of the Olympian gods. As Zeus grew into manhood, he learned about the horrible fate of his brothers and sisters who had come before him and he made up his mind to remedy the situation. Conspiring with his grandmother, Gaea, the young god secretly fed Cronos a dose of very strong medicine that made the king of the Titans feel nauseous. Presently, Cronos began vomiting up all those he had swallowed. First came the stone that had been substituted for Zeus, an object that humans later found and placed in the sacred sanctuary of Delphi, in central Greece.[9] Then out popped Cronos's and Rhea's first five children, all now grown into adults like Zeus. These were Hestia (the Roman Vesta), Demeter (the Roman Ceres), Hera (the Roman Juno), Hades (or Pluto; the Romans also called him Pluto, as well as Dis), and Poseidon (the Roman Neptune).

Rhea hands Cronos a rock wrapped in swaddling clothes. According to Greek mythology, Cronos believed the rock was his sixth child, Zeus, and the dim-witted Titan proceeded to swallow it.

Zeus and his five sisters and brothers immediately joined forces and waged war on Cronos and most of the other Titans; but after ten years of this battle for the universe, neither side had managed to get the upper hand. It was then that one of the Titans, Prometheus, whose name means "forethought," advised Cronos to release his monstrous brethren from Tartarus. With the hundred-handed creatures and the Cyclopes fighting on their side, said Prometheus, they might gain the advantage over the enemy. But Cronos showed his stupidity once more by refusing to take this advice.

So the frustrated Prometheus, along with his brother Epimetheus (meaning "afterthought"), abandoned Cronos and went over to Zeus's side. Prometheus gave Zeus the same advice about releasing the monsters, and Zeus, who was a good deal smarter than Cronos, did so. After ages of imprisonment, the Cyclopes, whose names were Thunderer, Lightener, and Shiner, were so grateful to be free that they each gave Zeus a present—the thunder, the lightning, and the thunderbolt, respectively. They also gave Hades a special cap that rendered him invisible while wearing it, and to Poseidon they presented a trident, or three-pronged spear, which became his symbol.

The war resumed with a frightful vengeance. Hesiod described it in the following way:

On that day they joined in hateful battle, all of them, both male and female, the Titan gods and those whom Cronos sired and those whom Zeus brought to light from . . . beneath the earth, strange, mighty ones, whose power was immense. . . . They stood against the Titans in the grim battle, with giant rocks in their strong hands, while on the other side the Titans eagerly strengthened their ranks. . . . The boundless sea roared terribly around, the great earth rumbled, and broad heaven groaned, shaken; and tall Olympus was disturbed down to its roots, when the immortals charged. The heavy quaking from their footsteps reached down to dark Tartarus, and piercing sounds of awful battle, and their mighty shafts.[10]

At last, after the forests had burned and the rivers boiled, Zeus and his forces were triumphant. They cast Cronos and most of the other Titans down into dark Tartarus, bounded by Styx, the black river

of death, and guarded by the Cyclopes, the hundred-handed ones, and also by a fearsome three-headed watchdog named Cerberus. Because they had helped Zeus, Prometheus and Epimetheus were allowed to remain free.

Dwellers on Olympus

Zeus and his companions now divided up the earth among themselves. They became known as the Olympians because they often dwelled in a magnificent palace high atop Mount Olympus. Zeus, who had led the rebellion, assumed over-lordship and took his sister Hera as his wife. Zeus not only ruled the gods and the earth but also became chief administrator of justice and protector of oaths sworn in his name. In addition to the thunderbolt, his symbols became his majestic throne,

Zeus, riding his mighty chariot, rages in battle against the Titans, whom the Olympians would eventually defeat and replace as lords of the earth.

his scepter, and the eagle. Though known for his justice and tremendous power (in the *Iliad* he boasts that in a tug of war he could easily best all the other Olympians put together), Zeus had his faults and vices, perhaps the worst being his tendency to lust after human women. On many later occasions he would descend to earth in disguise and have love affairs; usually Hera would find out and achieve her revenge by punishing the mortal women involved. Out of her constant concern for the sanctity of marriage, she appropriately became the guardian of that institution and also of childbirth. The cow and the peacock were sacred to her, and the Greeks often pictured her wearing or holding a wedding veil.

The Sacred Mountain

In this excerpt from his book An Introduction to Greek Mythology, *scholar David Bellingham describes how the classical Greeks showed their piety by dedicating temples and statues on and near Mount Olympus, in the central Greek region of Thessaly, which they held to be the abode of the gods.*

"Most Greek myths and legends had geographical locations in the real Greek world and covered the whole of the Mediterranean region. . . . Perhaps the most famous location is Mount Olympus, the mythical home of the Olympian gods. Its snowy peaks are rarely visible, often shrouded in clouds which added to the sense of awe felt by the Greeks towards this most sacred of places. Archaeologists have recently discovered a ruined temple on the summit (at 9,186 ft/2,800 m), almost certainly dedicated to Zeus, the king of the Olympian gods. It is unlikely that this inhospitably sited temple was often used for worship, but remains of animal sacrifices, dedicatory inscriptions, and coins have been found in the recent excavations. It was linked by a sacred way to the city of Dion, down in the valley; here there were many rich temples dedicated to various Olympians. A statue of Dionysus, not one of the original twelve Olympians, and a temple of the Egyptian goddess Isis have also been found; the temple of Isis was built during the later Hellenistic period [the third through first centuries B.C.] when the Greek world had expanded to embrace alien cultures and their religions. Dion was also the original location of the Olympic Games, organized in honor of Zeus, before they were transferred in the 8th century B.C. to Olympia [in southern Greece]."

Meanwhile, Zeus's brothers acquired their own, although lesser, realms. Poseidon took control of the sea. He was also the bringer of earthquakes, hence his frequent title "Earthshaker," and because he ended up giving humanity its first horse, he also became the god of horses. About Poseidon, classical scholar David Bellingham says:

> His adventures often resemble those of Zeus, involving the seduction of mortal women in the guise of animals, including a ram, a dolphin, and a bird. . . . Poseidon was constantly fighting for dominion of places on the land, including Athens, which he lost to his niece Athena. . . . In art he is similar to Zeus, perhaps lacking his more domineering attitude, and identifiable by his trident; sometimes he holds a sea-creature.[11]

Hades became ruler of the underworld, from which he only rarely departed to visit Olympus or the earth's surface. Although he ruled harshly and with little pity, he was not an evil god and was known for his sense of justice.

The Family of Gods

Zeus's sisters had their own important roles. Hestia, who remained always a virgin, became protector of the hearth and home and in Greek families every meal began and/or ended with a prayer or offering to her. Also, every town honored her with a public hearth in which the fire was never extinguished. In Rome, where she was called Vesta, her sacred fire was tended by priestesses known as the Vestals,

Demeter, whom the Romans called Ceres, bears her symbolic sheaf of wheat. She revealed her secret rites and "awful mysteries which no one may in any way transgress" to Triptolemus of Eleusis.

who were, like the goddess, virgins. Her sister Demeter oversaw agriculture and later, when humans began to worship her, the chief festival in her honor was at harvesttime. After Demeter's daughter, Persephone (or Prosperina), was abducted into the underworld by Hades, Demeter left Olympus and dwelled thereafter on earth, often inside the sacred temple the Greeks erected to her in Eleusis, west of Athens.

The God Who Made People Merry

Dionysus, son of Zeus and a mortal woman named Semele, was god of the vine, wine, fertility, and the endless cycle of the seasons. Not among the original Olympians, he was, according to legend, the last god to make his home on Mount Olympus. Here, from her classic book, Mythology, *noted scholar Edith Hamilton explains one reason that Dionysus, also known as Bacchus, was special to so many residents of the classical world.*

"The worship of Dionysus was centered in . . . two ideas so far apart--of freedom and ecstatic joy and of savage brutality. The God of Wine could give either to his worshipers. Throughout the story of his life he is sometimes man's blessing, sometimes his ruin. . . . The reason that Dionysus was so different at one time from another was because of [the] double nature of wine [it makes people feel happy but also causes them to get drunk and feel sick] and so of the god of wine. . . . On his beneficent side he was not only the god that makes men merry. His cup was 'Life-giving, healing every ill.' Under his influence courage was quickened and fear banished, at any rate for the moment. He uplifted his worshipers; he made them feel that they could do what they thought they could not. All this happy freedom and confidence passed away, of course, as they either grew sober or got drunk, but while it lasted it was like being possessed by a power greater than themselves. So people felt about Dionysus as about no other god. He was not only outside of them, he was within them, too. They could be transformed by him into being like him. . . . They could themselves [if only briefly] become 'divine.'"

Dionysus, also called Bacchus, reclines holding his characteristic wine goblet. According to legend, he wandered across the earth teaching people how to make wine.

Hermes, whom the Romans knew as Mercury, carries his symbolic staff. The Greeks believed that he guided the spirits of the dead to the underworld. They also credited him with inventing the alphabet, mathematics, astronomy, and boxing.

Though Demeter seemed to have abandoned Olympus, a number of other important gods soon came to reside there. Aphrodite, goddess of love, who had earlier risen from the sea foam that grew from Cronos's blood droplets, was one of them.[12] Depending on the situation, she showed one of the two sides of her personality—the first side soft, lovely, and pleasant, befitting her stunning physical beauty, and the second side spiteful, calculating, and malicious, as when she manipulated males, both mortal and immortal. Her favorite tree was the myrtle, and her chosen bird the dove.

Most of the other powerful Olympians were Zeus's children. These included Ares (the Roman Mars), god of war, whose bird, the vulture, befitted his hateful, ruthless personality;[13] stately Athena (the Roman Minerva), goddess of wisdom and war and protector of civilized life, who sprang fully clothed in armor from Zeus's head, and who later became the patron deity of Greece's greatest city—Athens; the incredibly handsome Apollo (the Romans called him this, too), lord of light, truth, the healing arts, and also of music and poetry, his symbol the laurel tree and his greatest shrine at Delphi, site of the famous oracle; swift and cunning Hermes (the Roman Mercury), the messenger god and patron of travelers, who also guided the souls of the dead to the underworld, his symbols his magic wand and winged cap and sandals; Apollo's twin sister, Artemis (the Roman Diana), goddess of the moon and the hunt, who also protected young girls and pregnant women, her symbol the cypress tree and her mascots deer and dogs; and Hera's son,[14] the kind and peace-loving Hephaestos (the Roman Vulcan), god of fire and forges and also patron of craftsmen.

The Creatures of Prometheus

In this bygone era when the Olympians wrested control of the world from the Titans and established themselves in their various roles, there were still no humans on earth. The Greeks told two different stories explaining the creation of people. In one, the gods made a series of human races, each succeeding race less admirable than

Hephaestos (the Roman Vulcan) works at his forge. He not only created the first woman from a lump of clay, but also fashioned Zeus's golden throne and shield, the latter causing storms and thunder when shaken.

its predecessors. Scholar Max J. Herzberg summarizes the ages of these early races:

> In the Golden Age . . . life was an eternal springtime. The soil brought forth so profusely that all toil was unnecessary. Men were both happy and good; old age came slowly. They dwelt always in the out-of-doors, and knew neither strife nor poverty. . . . Next came the Silver Age [in which Zeus created the seasons, making labor necessary]. Hunger and cold prevailed, and houses had to be built. Man in that age showed courage, but he was often overbearing and forgot to pay due reverence to the gods. The Age of Silver was followed by the Age of Bronze, in which men learned the use of arms and made war upon one another. Last was the Age of Iron—an era of crime and dishonor, when the gifts of the gods were misused and mankind sank into utter degradation.[15]

The classical Greeks believed that they lived in the unwholesome Age of Iron, in which the passing of generations seemed always to produce sons inferior to their fathers. They looked back with awe and longing to the Age of Bronze, an era of admirable and stalwart heroes of old.[16]

The more popular story for the creation of humans involved the Titans Prometheus and Epimetheus, who had been allowed their freedom after the great war. Prometheus was very wise—supposedly the wisest of all gods—and for that reason served for many years as Zeus's adviser. Duly impressed with Prometheus's abilities, Zeus delegated to him and his brother the task of making races of mortal animals and humans. Unfortunately, the scatterbrained Epimetheus, living up to the name Afterthought, acted without thinking and gave most of the choicest physical traits, including swiftness, strength, fur, wings, protective shells, and so on, to the animals so that when the time came to make humans, little was left that would help them to survive in a hostile world.

Prometheus tried hard to find a way to rectify his brother's mistake. First, he fashioned some humans from mud still containing sparks of life left over from Chaos, which had not yet completely sorted itself out. As an initial special gift to set them apart from the animals, Prometheus endowed the mud creatures with the physical form of the divine gods. But this trait was clearly not enough. He observed that

In this famous seventeenth-century painting, Prometheus carries fire from heaven, bent on introducing it to humanity. For this transgression, Zeus inflicted on him a terrible punishment.

these unfortunate mortals had to struggle hard, not only against wild beasts, but also against harsh extremes of weather. Life would be so much better for them, he reasoned, if only they possessed fire and understood how to use it. So Prometheus approached Zeus with the idea of giving humans the gift of fire. "No!" the king of the gods declared bluntly. "These creatures are not worthy of the divine spark of fire and they shall not have it."

But though Zeus had forbidden it, Prometheus decided to give his precious creations fire anyway. The former Titan snatched a bit of fire from the sun and hid it in a hollow reed, which he carried with him to earth. He taught the humans the uses of fire, including how to cook their food; to make weapons for defense; and to fashion tools to make houses, ships, utensils, and all manner of other things. Prometheus also taught people the use of the calendar, how to write, and some of the healing arts.

The Wrath of Zeus

When Zeus saw that Prometheus had disobeyed him and that humans were beginning to build an impressive civilization, he was very angry. The chief Olympian made up his mind to punish both the humans and the Titan, and in that order. Zeus noticed that all of the "creatures of Prometheus" were of a single gender—all of them men; and he devised a plan to introduce among them a second gender, one that would seem very charming but whose devious and manipulative nature would cause them trouble and grief. According to noted classical scholar W. H. D. Rouse:

[Zeus] sent for Hephaestos, the clever craftsman, and told him to make a woman. . . . Hephaestos took a lump of clay and molded it into the shape of one of the immortal goddesses. He molded a beautiful creature . . . and all the gods and goddesses gave their gifts. The goddess Athena dressed her in fine clothes and taught her spinning, and weaving, and needlework. Aphrodite . . . filled her with grace, and made her such that every man would wish her to be his own. . . . Hermes put lovely speech into her mouth and all sorts of trickery into her mind.

They named her Pandora, or All-gifts, because all the gods and goddesses had brought her a gift. Then Zeus sent Hermes to take Pandora down to earth and to give her to Epimetheus.[17]

Prometheus had warned his brother not to accept any gifts from Zeus, but Epimetheus, as usual, acted without thinking. He welcomed Pandora into his home as his wife, along with a large sealed jar she had been told was her dowry, although she was unsure of the container's contents. Eventually, her curiosity got the better of her, and with Epimetheus's help

---

Hephaestos Chains Prometheus

The play Prometheus Bound, *by Aeschylus, depicts the beginning of the Titan's punishment as he is chained to a rock on the summit of Mount Caucasus. In this speech from the opening scene (in the E. H. Plumptre translation in* Nine Greek Dramas*), Hephaestos, who has been ordered by Zeus to bind Prometheus, expresses his great reluctance to do so.*

"My courage fails to bind a god of my own kin by force to this bare rock where tempests wildly sweep; and yet I needs must muster courage for it: It's no slight thing the Father's [Zeus's] words to scorn. . . . [(to Prometheus)] Against my will I fetter you against your will with bonds of bronze that none can loose, to this lone height where you shall know neither voice nor face of man, but scorching in the hot blaze of the sun, shall lose your skin's fair beauty. You shall long for starry-mantled night to hide day's sheen . . . and evermore the weight of present ill shall wear you down. . . . This [is] the fate you gain as due reward for your philanthropy [giving humans the gift of fire]. For you, a God not fearing wrath of Gods, in your transgression gave their power to men; and therefore on this rock of little ease you still shall keep your watch, never lying down, never knowing sleep, never ever bending knee; and many groans and wailings profitless your lips will utter; for the mind of Zeus remains inexorable [unyielding]."

An engraving shows Prometheus, bound to a rock, unable to defend himself as a huge vulture prepares to peck at his liver and other organs. The fifth-century Greek writer Aeschylus tells this story in his play Prometheus Bound.

she broke the seal and opened the jar. Immediately, out rushed a swirling torrent of evils—diseases, worries, pitilessness, and all the other troubles that plague humanity to this day, for once they had been loosed from the jar, they could never be forced back in. Thus did Zeus accomplish the first part of his punishment.

Zeus aimed the second part of his wrath at Prometheus, who had had the gall to bring down fire from heaven. At Zeus's order, two giants seized the Titan, and Hephaestos, much against his kindly nature, bound him to a huge rock on the summit of a faraway mountain. There, each day a gigantic eagle (in some ver-

sions a vulture) gnawed at Prometheus's liver. At night, when the bird was gone, the liver grew back, and the next day the chained god had to endure the same agonies again.[18]

One version of these tales holds that Pandora's unleashing of troubles on humankind and Prometheus's grisly tortures were not enough to quench Zeus's anger. Only by destroying humanity once and for all would the chief god be satisfied, so he caused an immense flood that threatened to overwhelm the entire earth. Luckily, Prometheus, though he was chained, still possessed the gift of foresight, and he managed to warn his son Deucalion about

New Life from Stones and Mud

This excerpt from the Metamorphoses *of the Roman poet Ovid [in Rhoda Hendricks's translation] describes how, after the great flood brought by Zeus, Deucalion and Pyrrha repopulated the earth.*

"They veiled their heads, loosened their garments, and threw the stones behind them as they had been ordered. The stones—who would believe this unless the great age of the story served as evidence?—began to lay aside their cold stiffness and to soften gradually and, when they had become soft, to take form. Soon, when they grew larger and their nature became less harsh, a certain human shape, still not clear, could be seen, but it was very much like rough figures beginning to be carved from marble and not well-defined. Then in a short time, by the divine will of the gods, the stones thrown from the man's hands took on the appearance of men, and women were created again from those stones thrown by the woman. This is the reason we are a tough race, a race that endures hard work, ever showing evidence of the origin of our being. The earth, of its own accord, brought forth other animals of different forms. Damp warmth brings all things to life. When, therefore, the earth, covered with mud from the recent flood, grew warm again from the nourishing heat of the sky's sunlight, she put forth countless kinds of living things. Some she brought back in their ancient forms, some she created as new and unfamiliar shapes."

the impending disaster. Deucalion and his wife, Pyrrha, climbed atop Mount Parnassus, near Delphi in central Greece, hoping to escape the rising waters. After all other humans had perished, Zeus's anger was at last extinguished and he took pity on the couple and allowed them to survive.[19] Soon afterward, on the advice of a mysterious voice, Deucalion and Pyrrha gathered together many small stones, veiled their heads, and walked along, casting the stones behind them as they went. The stones he cast grew into men, and the stones she tossed grew into women; and in this way they repopulated the earth.

Thus with the transformation of Chaos into order and the birth of Gaea and Uranus, who gave rise to the Titans, who themselves produced the Olympians; the great war in which the Olympians emerged victorious; the rise of the creatures of Prometheus and the gift of fire he gave them; and finally the great flood and rise of a new race of humans, at long last the creation of the earth and heavens and the gods and mortals was complete.

Chapter

2 Men Who Lived for Action and Glory: The Trojan War

To the classical Greeks, the Trojan War represented much more than a collection of exciting adventure tales from a dimly remembered yet awe-inspiring bygone age. The later Greeks firmly believed that the war had been a real event, that those who waged it had been real people, and that these earlier Greeks had been both more blessed and more admirable than later Greeks. They had been more blessed because, as Homer's *Iliad* recorded, they frequently experienced direct contact with various gods who intervened in their lives. And the earlier Greeks had been more admirable because they had banded together, men from many different kingdoms and cities, and fought against the Trojans as a united army. By contrast, the classical Greek city-states (which saw themselves as separate nations) were notorious for their inability to get along and almost constantly fought among themselves. Above all, noted scholar C. M. Bowra points out, the classical Greeks believed that their ancestors who had fought the Trojan War "had been a race of supermen, of heroes, who were endowed physically and mentally beyond the common lot and who lived for action and the glory which it brings, especially through prowess in battle."[20]

It is not surprising, then, that the stories of the Trojan War, which depicted early religious, patriotic, and heroic ideals, became a kind of Greek national epic. The most famous and important of these stories were the more than fifteen-thousand-line *Iliad*, which describes the exploits of the Greek warrior Achilles during the tenth and final year of the war, and the twelve-thousand-line *Odyssey*, about the wanderings of another Greek warrior, Odysseus, after the war. According to classical historian Michael Grant, these two epic poems

> supplied the Greeks with their greatest civilizing influence, and formed the foundation of their literary, artistic, moral, social, educational and political attitudes. . . . They attracted universal esteem and reverence, too, as sources of general and practical wisdom, as arguments for heroic yet human nobility and dignity, as incentives to vigorous . . . manly action, and as mines of endless quotations and commentaries: the common property of all Greeks everywhere.[21]

As the ancient world gave way to the modern, the *Iliad* and *Odyssey* also gained the distinction of being the only surviving parts of a larger, so-called Trojan cycle of epics. There were originally at least six others: the *Cypria*, describing events leading up to the war; the *Aethiopis, Little Iliad,* and

Sack of Troy, about incidents of the war itself; the *Nostoi*, recounting the homecomings of the victorious Greeks; and the *Telegony*, about the exploits of Odysseus's son Telegonus.[22] The lost epics likely inspired retellings of various episodes by many post-Homeric ancient writers, including Aeschylus, Euripides, the second-century B.C. Greek Apollodorus, and Virgil. These retellings, along with the two surviving epics, particularly the *Iliad*, form the basis of the Trojan War story familiar today.

The Judgment of Paris

The singular events leading up to the great ten-year siege of Troy began when Eris, the ornery minor deity of discord, found that she had not been invited, as the major Olympian gods had, to a sumptuous banquet honoring the marriage of the sea nymph Thetis (mother of the hero Achilles). To exact her revenge for this slight, Eris flew over the banquet hall and tossed in a golden apple. The apple was marked "for the fairest goddess of all," and not surprisingly each of the goddesses present thought the bauble was intended for her. Eventually, Hera, Aphrodite, and Athena stepped forward and asked Zeus to choose which of them should get to keep the golden apple; but Zeus, who did not relish having to deal with the scorn of the two losers, wisely refused to act as judge.

Zeus claimed he had a better idea. There was a young man named Paris, he said, a prince of the powerful city of Troy on the northwestern coast of Asia Minor (now Turkey), who was known to be an excellent judge of beauty. Zeus persuaded the goddesses to go to Mount Ida, near

Troy, and seek out the youth. The three competitors soon found Paris tending sheep on Ida's slopes. Not long before, his father, King Priam, having heard a prophecy that the young man would one day bring about Troy's ruin, had ordered Paris out of the city.

Paris was very surprised when the three goddesses appeared before him. Wasting no time, each attempted to bribe him into choosing her. Hera promised to make him the ruler of all Europe and Asia, Athena said she would make him the victor in a war in which his Trojans would defeat the Greeks, and Aphrodite offered to make the most beautiful woman in the world fall in love with him. It was a difficult choice, but in the end Paris opted for love, and Aphrodite, having won the contest, received the coveted golden apple.

As everyone at that time knew well, the most beautiful of all mortal women was Helen, wife of Menelaus, king of the Greek kingdom of Sparta. She was so attractive, in fact, that all of the Greek kings and princes had once professed their love for her; and when she and Menelaus were betrothed, her father had made them all swear that they would help Menelaus if any of them broke up his marriage. Aphrodite led Paris to Sparta, where he became a guest of the unsuspecting royal couple. A while later, after Menelaus had left on a trip to Crete, the Trojan prince convinced Helen to run away with him and she and Paris escaped one night, leaving behind the queen's nine-year-old daughter.

When Menelaus returned from Crete, explained Apollodorus in his *Bibliotheca*, and

> learned that Helen had been carried off, he went to Mycenae [a powerful

A drawing of the famous sculpture of Helen of Troy at Salonica, in northern Greece. Renowned for her incomparable beauty, she has been the subject of numerous statues, paintings, poems, plays, and films.

kingdom located northeast of Sparta] to urge Agamemnon [king of Mycenae and Menelaus's brother] to gather together an army to go against Troy and to raise troops throughout Greece. He himself, sending a herald to each one of the kings, reminded them of the oath they had taken to come to his aid in case anyone wronged him in regard to his marriage. And he advised each of them to watch out for the safety of his own wife, telling them that the insult was shared in common by all of Greece.[23]

Odysseus's Reluctance to Go to War

A number of stories tell of the preparations for the Greek expedition against Troy. One of the them concerns Odysseus (whom the Romans called Ulysses), the wily king of the island kingdom of Ithaca, off Greece's western coast. At first he did not want to waste his time and resources in a war over another man's wife, especially now that he was very happy with his own wife, Penelope; so when the call went out for the Greek forces to gather, he ignored it. Eventually, Agamemnon, who had been named the leader of the Greek host, sent the wise Palamedes to Ithaca to persuade Odysseus. When Palamedes arrived, the Ithacan king pretended to be insane, harnassing an ox and a donkey to his plow and sowing salt into the sand on a beach. But Palamedes saw through the ruse and placed Odysseus's young son Telemachus directly in the plow's path. Odysseus immediately veered away, of course, an act that saved the boy but at the

How Troy's Great Walls Were Built

In one of the myths related to Troy, Zeus early helped set the stage for the Trojan War by ordering the gods Apollo and Poseidon to spend a year working for Laomedon, then the Trojan king. Laomedon had the two Olympians build the city's towering walls, sure that this would make it invulnerable to attack. In his Olympian Odes *(translated by Rhoda Hendricks in* Classical Gods and Heroes*), the poet Pindar wrote:*

"When Apollo, the son of Leto, and Poseidon . . . were going to build walls around the city of Troy, they called upon Aeacus [Achilles' grandfather] to help them in the work. . . . When the walls were just newly built, three gleaming serpents sprang upon the fortifications. But two fell back and died in amazement, whereas the third swiftly went over the wall with a loud noise. Apollo, turning over this adverse portent [omen] in his mind, said, 'The citadel of Troy is overpowered, Aeacus, at the place where your [mortal] hands have worked. A sign sent from loud-thundering Zeus the son of Cronos tells me this. This will not happen without your sons, however, for the capture of Troy will begin with the first generation of your descendants and will continue until the fourth generation.' Thus, in truth, the god Apollo spoke plainly and then set out toward Xanthus. And Poseidon, the wielder of the trident, drove off in his swift chariot toward Isthmus on the sea, taking Aeacus with him in his chariot of gold."

Apollo, god of the sun and of music and poetry, sits with his most famous invention, the lyre.

same time showed that Odysseus was perfectly rational and in control. Giving in, he assembled twelve ships and some six hundred men and sailed with Palamedes to Aulis, on Greece's eastern coast, where the Greek forces were gathering.

Achilles

In the meantime, another well-known Greek attempted to avoid the expedition. He was Achilles, Thetis's son, and without doubt the greatest warrior in Greece. When he was an infant, his divine mother had dipped him into the River Styx, which had made his body invulnerable to wounds, all except the heel she held while lowering him into the dark waters. It was essential that Achilles join the expedition in order to fulfill a prophecy declaring that Troy would never fall in his absence; yet an oracle had issued another prophecy, this one warning that he would surely die in a war against the Trojans. "To keep her son out of the Greek army," Max Herzberg explains:

> Thetis sent the young hero to stay with his uncle, who was bidden to disguise him in women's clothes. Odysseus learned where he was hiding, and went to the palace as a peddler. On his trays were many articles such as appeal to women, but mingled with them were a sword and a buckler [a small round shield]. As he spread out his wares before the royal maidens, he noticed that one of them disregarded the ribbons and the linens and fingered the sword eagerly. So he discovered Achilles, and in a little while he persuaded him to accompany him back to Aulis.[24]

Iphigenia's Sacrifice

A thousand ships had gathered in Aulis, and at last it was time to depart for the voyage across the Aegean Sea to Troy. But the Greeks soon discovered that it was impossible to leave the port because of a powerful north wind that kept on blowing day after day. A soothsayer finally communicated the words of the goddess Artemis, who was enraged that Agamemnon had recently hunted down and slain some woodland creatures sacred to her. To appease her, she said, Agamemnon would have to sacrifice his eldest daughter, Iphigenia; otherwise, the ships would never make it out of Aulis. Agamemnon loved his daughter, but as a king and commander of so large an army, he held the expedition's importance above hers and decided he had no choice but to do as the goddess bid. In his play *Agamemnon*, Aeschylus captured the horror of the poor girl's last moments:

> "My father, father!"—she might pray to the winds; no innocence moves her judges mad for war. Her father called his henchmen on, on with a prayer: "Hoist her over the altar like a yearling, give it all your strength! She's fainting—lift her, sweep her robes around her, but slip this strap in her gentle curving lips . . . here, gag her hard, a sound will curse the house [of Atreus, Mycenae's royal family]"—and the bridle chokes her voice . . . her saffron robes pouring over the sand, her glance like arrows showering, wounding every murderer through with pity clear as a picture.[25]

Thus did innocent Iphigenia die and Artemis withdrew the winds, allowing the

Artemis (the Roman Diana) stands in her chariot, which is pulled by two women. Her anger over Agamemnon's transgression led to the sacrifice of young Iphigenia.

Greek armada to sail forth for Troy. But Agamemnon and other members of his royal house would later pay a terrible price for the young girl's sacrifice.

Zeus's Intervention

When the Greeks reached the flat and windy plain of Troy, which separated the city's towering and well-fortified walls from the beaches, they were confident of a swift victory. After all, they not only greatly outnumbered the Trojans, but also possessed many distinguished war leaders. In addition to Agamemnon, Menelaus, Odysseus, and Achilles, there were Ajax, a prince of the island of Salamis, renowned for his enormous size and strength; Nestor, an old sage and the king of Pylos; the skilled warrior Diomedes, king of Argos; and Patroclus, Achilles' brave friend and attendant.

Yet the Trojans had their own heroes. First and foremost among these was Hector, Priam's son and Paris's brother, the most fearsome warrior in the Aegean sphere next to Achilles. Other Trojan assets included Troilus, another of Priam's sons, and Aeneas, reputed to be the son of the goddess Aphrodite and a mortal man named Anchises. Not only did the Trojans fight bravely and well under these leaders, but Troy's massive walls proved a formidable barrier and the initial Greek attacks were repulsed with heavy casualties. Consequently, Agamemnon's forces settled down, constructed a more permanent camp, and laid siege to the city.

For nine long years the war dragged on with neither side able to achieve a clear advantage. And during these years, many of the Olympian gods took sides in the conflict. Because Paris had helped Aphrodite acquire the golden apple, and also because her son, Aeneas, resided in Troy, she backed the Trojan cause, as did the war god Ares. Naturally enough, Hera and Athena, still resentful over losing the

Halfway Between Gods and Men

In this excerpt from his book Myths of the Greeks and Romans, *respected classical scholar Michael Grant examines the image of the hero created in the stories of the Trojan War, especially the* Iliad, *a societal, ethical, and literary concept readily accepted and perpetuated by the post-Homeric Greeks.*

"The hero must use his superior qualities at all times to excel and win applause, for that is the reward and demonstration of his manhood. He makes honor his paramount code, and glory the driving force and aim of his existence. Birth, wealth and prowess confirm a hero's title; his ideals are courage, endurance, strength and beauty. Enthusiastically confident in what he achieves and possesses, he relies upon his own ability to make the fullest use of his powers. Yet, although he is no god, there is something about him which brings him not too far from heaven: Hesiod thought of the heroes as half-way between gods and men. Their mighty achievements inspired poets to suggest that human nature, far though it is from divinity, can yet come within reach of it. . . . The Hero [as depicted in the *Iliad*] has transformed our ways of thinking. The heroic outlook shook off primitive superstitions and taboos by showing that man can do amazing things by his own effort and by his own nature, indeed that he can almost rise *above* his own nature into strengths scarcely known or understood. As early as the Homeric poems themselves the great stories were held up as educational examples. This continued throughout antiquity [ancient times], and then again in the schools of the Renaissance, on which the . . . [educational, political, and military] institutions of today, not least in Britain and America, are still based."

judgment of Paris, favored the Greeks. By contrast, Apollo helped one side, then the other, and Zeus attempted to remain neutral, although he sometimes found himself drawn into the action.

One of these times was in the tenth year of the siege. Achilles and Agamemnon had a terrible quarrel, after which Achilles retired to his tent and refused to come out and lead the Greeks in battle as he had so often done. Believing that her noble son had been gravely insulted, Thetis approached Zeus and asked him to help her exact revenge. "O Father Zeus!" she cried out, according to Homer:

> If ever I have served you by word or deed, grant me this boon: give honor to my son! He of all others is to die an early death, but now see how my Lord Agamemnon has insulted him. . . . Satisfy my son, Zeus Olympian most wise! Let the Trojans prevail, until the Greek nation shall satisfy my son and magnify

him with honor!" Zeus Cloudgatherer did not answer, but long sat silent; and Thetis—how she clasped his knees, how she clung fast to him and cried out once more: "Say yes now, and promise me faithfully! Or else say no—for you have nothing to fear!"[26]

Although reluctant to take sides, Zeus gave in to Thetis's request. Knowing full well that the Greeks would be at a distinct military disadvantage without Achilles in their ranks, he urged Agamemnon in a dream to attack while Achilles was indisposed. Agamemnon did so and a great battle ensued. At one point during the fighting, the ranks of the two armies separated to watch an individual combat between Menelaus and Paris, whose rivalry for Helen had instigated the war. Paris's skills as a warrior were much inferior to Menelaus's, of course, and the Trojan prince would surely have been killed; however, at the crucial moment Aphrodite intervened and

Approached by Agamemnon's representatives, Achilles (sitting with lyre) refuses to fight, while his friend Patroclus (leaning on table) looks on.

Many scholars believe that the right hand of this bronze statue of Zeus, now in the Greek National Museum in Athens, once held an upraised thunderbolt.

saved him. Then mighty Hector entered the fray and led the Trojans in an irresistible offensive that drove the Greeks back nearly to their beach encampment.

The Fates of Patroclus and Hector

Pressed hard by the Trojan forces, the Greeks were now in a perilous position, and in despair Agamemnon proposed that his own army give up the fight and return to Greece. The events of the following day only seemed to confirm that this would be the best course. The Trojans crashed through the stockade protecting the Greek camp and forced many of the Greeks to retreat to their ships. Hector was seriously wounded by the powerful Ajax, but the healing god Apollo soon revived the Trojan champion, making him stronger than ever. "Aflame from head to foot" is how Homer described Hector at that moment. "Picture a wave raised by a gale and sweeping forward under the scudding clouds. It breaks on a gallant ship . . . and the crew . . . are left trembling and aghast. This is how Hector fell upon the Greeks, striking panic into their hearts." Triumphantly, he led his men to the Greek ships and shouted, "Bring fire, and raise the war-cry, all of you together. Zeus is repaying us for everything today: the ships are ours!"[27]

At this fateful juncture, with the Greek cause seemingly lost, brave Patroclus

The Struggle over Patroclus

This excerpt from Book XVII of the Iliad *(E. V. Rieu's translation) describes the fierce battle between the Greeks and Trojans for the body of the fallen hero Patroclus.*

"Menelaus and [the young archer] Meriones labored to retrieve Patroclus's body from the [battle]field and bring it to the hollow ships, with the battle raging round them, fierce as a fire that in a moment blazes up, falls on a town and consumes the houses in a mighty conflagration. As the roaring wind beats on the flames, so did the ceaseless din from fighting men and horses beat upon them as they went. They struggled along with their burden like mules who put out all their strength to drag a log or some huge timber for a ship down from the mountains by a rocky track, tugging away till they nearly break their hearts, what with the labor and the sweat. Behind them the two Aiantes [Aias of Salamis and Aias of Locris] held the enemy, as a wooded ridge that stretches out across the countryside holds back the floods. . . . Thus all the time the two Aiantes fended off the Trojans who attacked the rear. But they were hard beset, and by two men in particular, Aeneas . . . and the illustrious Hector. . . . The Greek warriors with cries of terror fled before Aeneas and Hector, losing all stomach for the fight; and many a fine weapon was dropped . . . by the fleeing Greeks, who were given no respite from attack."

approached Achilles, who was still brooding in his tent and refusing to fight. If Achilles would not enter the fray, said Patroclus, "at least allow *me* to take the field at once with the Myrmidon force [Achilles' own handpicked and much-feared warriors] at my back." Then Patroclus added, "And lend me your own armor to put on my shoulders so that the Trojans may take me for you and break off the battle, which would give our weary troops time to recuperate. Even a short breathing-space makes all the difference in war."[28]

Achilles agreed to Patroclus's request, and Patroclus, wearing his friend's armor, led the Myrmidons and other Greeks against the Trojans. Thinking that mighty Achilles himself was attacking them, the fearful Trojans began to fall back; even Hector could not withstand the force of the seemingly rejuvenated Greek army. But eventually, the overconfident Patroclus found himself face-to-face with Hector, who was much the superior warrior. Hector slew Patroclus and stripped off Achilles' armor, while, after a desperate struggle for the body, the Greeks bore Patroclus back to their ships.

Hearing of his friend's death, the grief-stricken Achilles became a changed man. His mother, Thetis, rushed to Hephaestos, who swiftly forged a new suit of armor for Achilles, this one even stronger and more beautifully ornamented than the one Patroclus had borrowed. Then Achilles went to Agamemnon and patched up their feud; wasting little time, he led his Myrmidons and the other Greeks in a mighty charge against the Trojan ranks.

Many of the gods, backing one side or the other, joined in the fray and, in Homer's own words:

> [They] drove the two hosts together and made the bitter strife burst forth. The Father of men and gods thundered terribly from on high, Poseidon made the solid earth quake from beneath, and the tall summits of the hills; Mount Ida shook from head to foot, and the citadel of Troy trembled, and the Greek ships [as well].[29]

In this painting by the seventeenth-century Flemish painter Anthony Van Dyck, Hephaestos presents Thetis with a new suit of armor for her son Achilles.

The Trojans, finally unable to withstand the Greek onslaught, fled back into the city; that is, with the exception of Hector, who stood alone outside the gates, waiting to face Achilles. The two champions engaged in mortal combat, Hector swinging his sword while "Achilles charged, the heart within him loaded with savage fury." As they circled each other, Achilles searched for an opening, somewhere on "Hector's splendid body" where he might thrust his spear. Finally, Hector's throat was momentarily exposed and "in this place brilliant Achilles drove the spear as he came on in fury, and clean through the soft part of the neck the spearpoint was driven." [30]

The Fall of Troy

The greatest Trojan warrior now lay dead in the dust before his horrified countrymen's eyes. Completing his vengeance, Achilles stripped off his opponent's armor, tied the corpse to the back of his chariot, and triumphantly dragged it around the city walls. In time, as his anger subsided, he agreed to give Hector's body to the grieving King Priam. The Trojans then conducted a solemn funeral for Hector while the Greeks held final rites for brave Patroclus.

After these ceremonies the war resumed, but with Hector dead and Achilles once more in the forefront of the Greek ranks, the Greeks appeared to have the advantage. Paris, an expert bowman, soon eliminated this advantage by shooting a poisoned arrow into Achilles' only vulnerable spot, his heel, killing the great warrior. But Paris did not live long enough to

gloat much over the deed, for the Greek warrior Philoctetes, using a special bow he had received from the renowned hero Heracles, felled and killed the Trojan prince. After this event, the siege continued to drag on.

Then the crafty Odysseus announced that he had a plan. In his *Aeneid*, Virgil told how:

> The Greek commanders had a horse constructed with ribs of interlocking planks of firewood. It stood high as a mountain. . . . They then drew lots and secretly hid selected troops inside its dark void, till its whole huge cavernous belly was stuffed with men at arms. . . . And thus far sailed the Greeks and hid their ships on [a nearby island's] desolate shore. [31]

Seeing the beaches empty and the Greek ships gone, the jubilant Trojans flooded forth from their city and danced on the windswept plain where so many valiant men from both sides had died. When they saw the huge wooden horse standing on one end of the plain, they wondered why the Greeks had built it. Then a Greek named Sinon stepped forth. He claimed that his countrymen had left him behind, angrily proclaimed that for this slight he no longer wanted to be a Greek, and finally explained that the great horse was intended as an offering to the goddess Athena.

Unfortunately for the Trojans, their leaders gullibly accepted this story, on which Odysseus had carefully coached Sinon, and ordered that the horse be dragged into the city. When it would not fit through the gates, the Trojans tore down part of a towering wall and through this

Searching for the Real Troy

While the ancient Greeks accepted that the Trojan War had been a real event, modern scholars of the eighteenth and nineteenth centuries believed that it and most of its characters were entirely mythical. Here, from his book The Legend of Odysseus, *classical historian Peter Connolly tells how the real Troy came to light at a site called Hisarlik, in what is now northwestern Turkey.*

"Troy was discovered by an amateur archaeologist, Heinrich Schliemann, in 1870. He found several towns each built on the ruins of the previous one. At the second level up he discovered signs of burning and concluded that this was Homer's Troy. In 1882 Schliemann was joined by a professional archaeologist, Wilhelm Dörpfeld, and the excavating was soon left to him. Dörpfeld identified nine successive towns on the site and was able to show that Homer's Troy was between the sixth and seventh levels. Dörpfeld's findings were checked by an American expedition between 1932 and 1938. They agreed with his findings but improved techniques enabled them to identify no less than 30 different levels of occupation. . . . Experts disagree over which Troy was destroyed by the Mycenaeans. . . . Troy VIIa was poor and overpopulated. It was destroyed by fire after a life of only about 30 years. Its crudely built houses were huddled against the town walls. . . . These features indicate a siege mentality, with the people from the countryside crowding into the town for protection."

After hearing the story of the Iliad *as a boy, Heinrich Schliemann became convinced that the Trojan War had been a real event.*

breach transported the prize into the heart of Troy. There they celebrated into the night until Troy became, in Virgil's words, a city "drowned in wine and sleep." And it was then that Odysseus sprang his trap. He and several of his comrades crawled from their hiding place in the belly of the horse. "They killed the sentries, they flung wide the gates, they admitted all their comrades," who had sailed back under the cover of darkness, and "they all joined forces." As a great slaughter began, "cries

In this woodcut from thirteenth-century Sicilian poet Guido delle Colonne's Trojan History, *the Trojans prepare to drag the famous wooden horse into their city.*

of agony arose louder and louder." The Trojan prince Aeneas later recalled:

> The clamor swelled and the horrible clash of combat. I started out of sleep and climbed to the rooftop . . . [and] saw only too clearly the naked treachery of the Greeks. . . . Men shouted, trumpets pealed. Out of my mind, I sprang to arms . . . more than to muster to me a band of fighters and rally with them to the citadel. Rage, fury mastered me; I had in my mind no thought but death in battle and its glory![32]

But the valiant efforts of Aeneas and other Trojan warriors were in vain. The city fell to the triumphant Greeks, who killed King Priam and all of the other Trojan leaders, save for Aeneas, who, bearing his aged father on his back and aided by his mother, Aphrodite, escaped into the countryside. The Greeks proceeded to loot the city, to burn it, and to carry away the surviving Trojan women as slaves. Meanwhile, Menelaus reclaimed Helen, whose matchlessly beautiful face, the bards would one day sing, had "launched a thousand ships." The prophecy that old Priam had feared and attempted to avert—namely, that his son Paris would bring about Troy's utter ruin—had finally and appallingly been fulfilled.

3 Jason, Odysseus, and Aeneas: Three Journeys of Epic Adventure

After the *Iliad*, the tales of Jason and the quest for the Golden Fleece, of Odysseus's search for his homeland, and of Aeneas and the Roman foundation were the most famous and most often retold of the large-scale mythical stories in ancient times. These three epics have much in common. First, they each involve a hero (or heroes) who embarks on a long journey on a ship (or ships) and ends up accomplishing a great goal. In the course of this journey, the hero sails through little-known waters, sometimes reaching what are to him the edges of the known world, and experiences many colorful, often dangerous adventures. And of course, as in most ancient myths, he encounters and is directly affected by the gods and other supernatural beings.

These tales also have in common the fact that the time periods in which they supposedly occurred neatly frame the momentous events of the Trojan War. Jason's adventures were thought to have taken place in the generation directly preceding the war. Many ancient writers produced versions of the quest for the Golden Fleece, among them Pindar in one of his odes and Apollonius of Rhodes in his almost six-thousand-line *Argonautica*, so named because Jason's ship was the *Argo* and its crew the Argonauts. The first-century A.D. Ro-

man epic poet Valerius Flaccus also wrote an *Argonautica* that has survived.[33]

By contrast, Odysseus's and Aeneas's adventures directly followed the events of the Trojan War. In fact, because both Odysseus and Aeneas were prominent players in that war, the fall of Troy acted as the springboard for these heroes' long journeys. The primary source for Odysseus's journey, of course, is Homer's *Odyssey*, and the principal ancient telling of Aeneas's adventures is Virgil's *Aeneid*. The *Aeneid* became the great patriotic national epic of the Roman people and a model and inspiration for later European epic poets such as Dante and Milton.

The One-Sandaled Man Appears

The famous quest for the Golden Fleece arose not long after an oracle had delivered a prophecy to Pelias, king of the powerful city of Jolcos, in Thessaly in central Greece. The oracle warned Pelias, who had earlier usurped the throne from his uncle, that he should beware of any stranger who arrived in Jolcos wearing only one sandal, for this man would cause Pelias to lose both his throne and his life. It

Publius Vergilius Maro (70–19 B.C.), popularly known as Virgil, produced the Aeneid, *the epic poem recounting the adventures of the Roman hero Aeneas.*

came to pass that just such a one-sandaled man appeared at the palace, having lost a sandal while crossing a flooded stream. He informed Pelias that he was his cousin Jason, son of the rightful king, and that he had come to claim his birthright and to bring enlightened rule to Jolcos, which Pelias had administered harshly.

Pelias deviously pretended to agree with Jason's claim to the throne, but secretly he plotted to rid himself of the young man. Pelias told Jason:

> You shall become king of Jolcos indeed, but first you must accomplish a special task. I am continually vexed by a spirit who bids me to bring the fabulous Fleece of the legendary Golden Ram back to Jolcos, its rightful home. At the moment, the Fleece hangs in a tree in the faraway land of Colchis and

since I am too old and weak to make the journey, you must do so. When you return with the Fleece, I swear by Father Zeus that I will abdicate and make you king.

This was a lie, of course. Pelias knew full well that the voyage to Colchis was long and extremely treacherous and that in all likelihood Jason would never return.

The *Argo*

But Jason felt confident that he could bring back the Fleece. To do so, he realized, he would need a special ship, and under the direction of the goddess Athena, the master shipbuilder Argus constructed the mighty *Argo*. According to Valerius Flaccus's account:

> A large gathering of men worked busily. At the same time . . . a grove of trees had been felled on all sides and the stores were resounding with the steady blows of the double-edged ax. Already Argus was cutting pines with the thin blade of a saw, and the sides of the ship were being fitted together. . . . Planks [were] being softened over a slow fire until they bent to the proper shape. The oars had been fashioned and Pallas Athena was seeking out a yardarm for the sail-carrying mast. When the ship stood finished, strong enough to plow through the pathless sea . . . Argus added varied ornamental paintings.[34]

Such a superior ship needed a superior crew and Jason soon gathered together many of the strongest, ablest, and noblest men of Greece. Among them were the mighty hero Heracles, accompanied by his faithful armor bearer Hylas; the master musician and singer Orpheus; the warrior Peleus (father of Achilles); Zeus's twin sons, Castor and Polydeuces (the Roman Pollux); and many others.

The Perilous Voyage to Colchis

Having stored sufficient provisions, Jason and his Argonauts finally embarked and sailed north. It was not long before they encountered their first setback, which took place near a pleasant bay where they had stopped for rest and exercise. As the noted nineteenth-century classical scholar Charles Kingsley told it:

> Heracles went away into the woods, bow in hand, to hunt wild deer; and Hylas the fair boy slipped away after him, and followed him by stealth, until he lost himself among the glens, and sat down weary to rest himself by the side of a lake; and there the water nymphs came up to look at him, and loved him, and carried him down under the lake to be their playfellow, forever happy and young. And Heracles sought for him in vain, shouting his name till all the mountains rang; but Hylas never heard him down under the sparkling lake. So while Heracles wandered searching for him, a fair breeze sprang up, and Heracles was nowhere to be found; and the *Argo* sailed away, and Heracles was left behind.[35]

Thus Heracles missed the Argonauts' subsequent adventures. These included

A statue of the goddess Athena holds a smaller sculpture of Nike, goddess of victory. According to legend, Athena oversaw the building of Jason's ship, the Argo.

narrowly making it through a channel bordered by the dreaded Clashing Rocks, which perpetually smashed together, destroying anything caught between them, and passing perilously near the country of the Amazons (daughters of the war god Ares), a tribe of fierce women warriors. They also sailed past the great rock on

Talos, the Bronze Giant

Some scholars have suggested that parts of the Argonaut story were based on dim memories of real events. In this excerpt from his book Lost Atlantis, *scholar J. V. Luce recalls an episode from the homeward voyage of the* Argo, *in which it encounters a giant named Talos, near Crete. Luce then relates various details of this legendary episode to the now-documented, large-scale eruption of the volcano on the island of Thera, also near Crete, in Minoan-Mycenaean times.*

"He [Talos] was made entirely of invincible bronze except for a vein near his ankle covered by a thin membrane. In terror of his missiles [the rocks he was throwing] the Argonauts backed away from the shore, and were about to sail on when Medea announced that she could overcome the giant. She cast a spell on him which had the effect of dimming his vision, and as he was levering up a great boulder to hurl at them, he grazed his ankle on a rocky pinnacle. 'Then the ichor [his life force] flowed out like molten lead,' and, losing strength rapidly, he fell from his rocky crag 'with a terrible crash.' Such is the story as told by Apollonius . . . writing in the third century B.C. But the Argonaut saga goes back to the earliest stages of Greek epic poetry, and has often been supposed to reflect early Mycenaean voyages of exploration. . . . What can we make of this bronze warder who hurls rocks at ships trying to sail to Crete? Is he simply a figure of folk-tale and imagination? . . . [Some scholars have] suggested that the figure of Talos embodies an early Greek memory of the Thera volcano. Thera 'guards' the northern approaches to Crete which would have been used by the early Mycenaean sailors. His frame of 'unbreakable bronze' represents the wall of the newly formed crater on the mountain peak of Thera as it then was. The rocks which he throws are the 'bombs' shot from the vent of the volcano. His 'heel' is a subsidiary volcano on the coast of the island. . . . He collapses and becomes quiescent when all his ichor has flowed out like 'molten lead'—a reminiscence of the cooling off of lava streams after the end of an eruption."

which Prometheus the Titan lay chained and heard the flapping of the wings of the giant eagle that plagued him.

In one particularly exotic and dangerous episode, the Argonauts tangled with the terrifying Harpies, flying creatures endowed with pointed beaks and claws and a sickening stench.[36] Jason and his men found an old man named Phineus, who was so starved and emaciated that all that was left of him was quite literally skin and bones. Apollo had once granted Phineus the gift of prophecy; but Zeus disapproved of humans knowing what he was going to do next and inflicted a punishment on the man. Every time Phineus began to eat a meal, the Harpies, sometimes called "Zeus's Hounds," would swoop down and cover his food with their stench, making it too disgusting to consume. In a courageous effort, some of the Argonauts succeeded in driving the Harpies away so that they never again bothered poor Phineus.

Fire-Breathing Bulls and Dragons' Teeth

Eventually, Jason and his crew reached the land of Colchis, on the far end of the Axine, or Unfriendly Sea.[37] There they asked the local king, Aeetes, to give them the Golden Fleece in exchange for which they would do him some important service, such as fighting his enemies. But Aeetes did not like foreigners and in any case was not about to give up the Fleece, so he concocted a plan that would surely result in Jason's death. No one could take the Fleece, Aeetes claimed, unless he first proved his courage through a formidable challenge. He would have to yoke two fearsome fire-breathing bulls and use them to plow dragons' teeth into the earth. These seeds would quickly grow into a multitude of armed warriors, whom he would have to defeat.

At first, it seemed to Jason that no mortal man could pass such a test, but he soon received some unexpected and formidable aid. The goddess Hera, who wanted Jason's quest to succeed, convinced Aphrodite to send her own son Eros (the Roman Cupid) to Colchis. Eros caused King Aeetes' daughter Medea almost instantly to fall in love with Jason, and, indeed, her love became so strong that she was willing to betray her own father for this Greek stranger. Medea, who possessed knowledge of sorcery, met Jason in secret and gave him a vial containing a magic drug. In Apollonius's version of the story, she gave Jason these instructions:

> At dawn, steep this drug in water, strip off naked, and rub it all over your body like oil: within it there'll be great strength and unlimited prowess—it's not men you'd think of matching yourself with, but the immortal gods. On top of this, see that your spear and shield are sprinkled, and your sword too: then you'll be proof against the spear-points of the earthborn men, against the irresistible onrush of flame from the deadly bulls.[38]

And sure enough, covered in this special ointment, Jason was able to yoke the bulls, defeat the seed-warriors, and thereby pass the test. Aeetes still did not want to give up the Fleece. But with more help from Medea, Jason managed to get past the huge serpent that guarded the Fleece and to spirit the prize out of Colchis and take it back to Greece.

Athena's Wrath

Once the Argonauts returned to Greece, they disbanded and some went on to further adventures of their own. Some had sons, who, when they grew into young men, joined the great Greek expedition against Troy that ended with that city's destruction. For example, Peleus's son Achilles became the war's most famous hero. But though the Greeks were victorious in the war, thanks in large degree to the help of various gods, many never made it home from the Trojan shores that had been their home for ten long years. The principal cause of this misfortune was that while the Greek soldiers were sacking the city, they went on a rampage during which some of them committed sacrilege. In particular, one of them broke into the local temple of Athena and dragged away King Priam's daughter Cassandra, who had invoked the goddess's protection by throwing her arms around her statue.

Athena was determined to make the Greeks pay for this outrage. She convinced Poseidon, who had sided with them during the war, to help her mete out punishment, and he proceeded to produce a tremendous storm that struck the Greek fleets as they were sailing homeward from Troy. The tempest was so violent that Agamemnon lost many of his ships, Menelaus was blown off course and ended up in Egypt, and hundreds of Greek sailors drowned.

One of the Greek leaders suffered much longer than the others—wily Odysseus, whose idea of the wooden horse had brought about Troy's downfall. In fact, his wanderings took him to many distant and exotic places, and it was fully ten years before he saw the shores of his native Ithaca again. In the tenth year of his travels, shortly before he made it home, Poseidon, still angry with him, wrecked the raft on which he was floating, and Odysseus washed ashore in the land of a friendly people called the Phaeacians. The

A drawing of eighteenth-century Danish sculptor Bertel Thorwaldsen's statue of the hero Jason holding the Golden Fleece, recently recovered from Colchis.

Phaeacian king, Alcinous, threw a banquet for the visitor, who told the story of his eventful and perilous ten-year journey.

"For nine days I was chased by those accursed winds across the fish-infested seas," Odysseus began. "But on the tenth we made [it to] the country of the Lotus-eaters, a race that live on vegetable foods." [39] The local inhabitants, he went on, gave some of his men some potent flower food, which made them feel lazy and forgetful and lose their desire to continue homeward. Odysseus finally had to resort to dragging these men back to the ships and chaining them to keep them from remaining forever in Lotus Land.

In the Cave of the Cyclops

Next, Odysseus recalled, "we came to the land of the Cyclopes, a fierce, uncivilized people, who never lift a hand to plant or plow, but put their trust in Providence." The Cyclopes' society is very different from that of civilized peoples, the storyteller explained. The people "have no assemblies for the making of laws, nor any settled customs, but live in hollow caverns in the mountain heights, where each man is lawgiver to his children and his wives, and nobody cares a jot for his neighbors." [40]

Because the one-eyed Cyclopes were so uncivilized, and also very large and powerful, the Greeks wanted to avoid contact with them. But Odysseus's men needed food. He took twelve of them ashore, and it was not long before they found a huge cave in which many sheep and goats were penned. But before the men could gather up the animals and de-part, the Cyclops who lived in the cave returned home. This crude giant, one Polyphemus by name, barred the entranceway with a gigantic rock. When he asked where the strangers had anchored their ship, Odysseus shrewdly answered that it had been wrecked in a storm and that he and these companions were the sole survivors. Polyphemus then abruptly and cruelly grabbed two of the Greeks, smashed them on the rocky floor until they were dead, and gulped them down for his supper.

The next morning, the Cyclops killed and ate two more of Odysseus's men and then left for the day, securing the great rock in the doorway so that the Greeks could not escape. When the giant returned that evening, he made still another meal of two men and then began to guzzle wine. In time, he demanded to know the Greek leader's name. Giving another shrewd reply, Odysseus claimed his name was "Nobody."

Later, the Cyclops fell asleep and Odysseus and his remaining men sharpened a wooden beam and heated it in the fire. Odysseus recalled:

[We] lifted it and rammed it deep in his crater eye, and I leaned on it, turning it as a shipwright turns a drill. . . . So with our brand we bored that great eye socket while blood ran out around the red hot bar. Eyelid and lash were seared; the pierced [eye]ball hissed broiling, and the roots popped. . . . The Cyclops bellowed and the rock roared round him. . . . Clawing his face he tugged the bloody spike out of his eye . . . [and] then he set up a howl for Cyclopes who lived in caves on windy peaks nearby. [41]

But when the other giants appeared outside the cave and asked, "What's wrong, Polyphemus? Who is hurting you?", he remembered the name Odysseus had given him and called out, "Nobody! Nobody is hurting me!" So the other Cyclopes, confused and a bit irritated, returned to their homes.

Numerous Adventures and Misfortunes

The next morning, the blinded Polyphemus had to roll back the huge rock to let his animals out to graze, giving the Greeks time to escape. The enraged Cyclops cried out to his father—who, unfortunately for Odysseus, happened to be Poseidon—to punish these men who had deceived and disfigured him. And Poseidon gladly did so.

The result was that Odysseus continued to wander for many years, encountering numerous adventures and misfortunes along the way. These included falling into the clutches of a race of giants, who ate all of his men except the crew of his own flagship; stopping at the isle of Aeaea, where the sorceress Circe changed half of his remaining men into pigs; sailing past the isle of the Sirens, deadly sisters whose deceptively lovely singing lured humans to their deaths; and weathering a mighty gale that killed all in the party except Odysseus himself. He ended up in a cave on a distant island ruled by the nymph Calypso, who kept him there for seven years, until

Sixteenth-century Italian artist Pellegrino Tibaldi's magnificent painting of Odysseus putting out the eye of the Cyclops Polyphemus.

This engraving on an Etruscan mirror shows Odysseus, sword drawn, demanding that the enchantress Circe restore his men, whom she has transformed into pigs.

finally Zeus took pity on him and ordered her to release him. It was not long afterward, Odysseus told his listeners at the banquet, that he had reached the Phaeacians' friendly shores.

After a short stay with these kindly people, Odysseus was delighted when King Alcinous offered to help him return to his beloved island of Ithaca. But when he landed there, he found his palace and family troubled. Because most Ithacans assumed that he had long since died, his wife, Penelope, was beset by over a hundred suitors, each of whom wanted to marry her for the money and titles he would get. After an emotional reunion with his now grown son Telemachus, Odysseus, disguised as a beggar, entered the palace banquet hall, where the suitors were gathered. He revealed himself to the startled men, and aided by Telemachus and two loyal servants, in a rage he began to fight and kill them. Homer dramatically described the death of one suitor, Eurymachus, this way:

He drew his sharp and two-edged sword of bronze, and leapt at Odysseus with a terrible shout. But at the same moment the brave Odysseus let an arrow fly, which struck him by the nipple on his breast with such force that it pierced his liver. The sword dropped from his hand. Lurching across the table, he crumpled up and tumbled with it, hurling the food and wine-cup to the floor. In agony he dashed his

The Navel of the Sea

In his fascinating book Ulysses Found, *noted scholar Ernle Bradford speculates about the actual locations within the Mediterranean sphere that, through popular sailors' tales, might have inspired various episodes of the* Odyssey. *In this excerpt Bradford suggests that the episode in which Odysseus (Ulysses) lived in a cave on Calypso's island was partially based on rumors about the then little known island we now call Malta.*

"The curious but distinctive description of Calypso's island as being the 'navel of the sea' can apply to only one place in the Mediterranean. Fifty miles south of Sicily, commanding the main channel through which all shipping must pass, the Maltese islands are almost equidistant from Gibraltar, on the one hand, and Cyprus on the other. Malta's importance as the finest harbor in the dead center of the Mediterranean sailing-routes was readily appreciated by the Phoenicians [a Middle Eastern people known for their maritime prowess]. . . . It is not surprising that the Phoenicians who first used the harbors of Malta were determined to keep the island a 'hidden place' from their rivals. There is nothing comparable to the Grand Harbor of Malta in the whole of this sea, and it is a natural harbor. . . . There is a further point which seems to establish the Phoenician connection between Calypso's cave and Malta. . . . Quite unlike the Greeks, who either buried or cremated their dead, the Phoenicians were in the habit of interring them in *caves*, usually horizontally, and with their feet towards the west. . . . Now the principal temples of Phoenician, as well as pre-Phoenician, Malta all have a cavelike appearance, even where they are not literally excavated out of the rock. With such an abundance of clues all pointing in the one direction, I cannot doubt that Malta was the island of Calypso."

forehead on the ground; his feet lashed out and overthrew the chair, and the fog of death descended on his eyes.[42]

Eventually, all of the suitors lay dead in the blood-soaked room. The honor of their royal house restored, at long last Odysseus and Penelope were reunited; and that night, the first they had spent together in twenty years, all hearts in Ithaca were filled with joy.

Aeneas Sails Westward

Unbeknownst to Odysseus, during his long wanderings to faraway and alien shores, another man who had fought at Troy was engaged in a similar journey of epic adventure. He was none other than stalwart Aeneas, the Trojan prince who had escaped from the burning city bearing old Anchises on his back. Gathering a few other Trojan survivors together into some ships, Aeneas sailed into the Aegean and one of his initial stops was the tiny sacred island of Delos. There, an oracle gave him a message from the god Apollo, saying that the Trojans should seek out their "ancient mother," the land from which their distant ancestors had originally come.

Believing this ancient motherland to be Crete, Aeneas led his followers to that large island lying southeast of the Greek mainland. But once there, they received another cryptic message from Apollo, this one informing them:

> There is a place the Greeks called Hesperia—the western land—an ancient country powerful in war and rich of soil. . . . [The inhabitants call] themselves "Italians" after Italus—one of their leaders. There lies your true home.[43]

Thus did Aeneas learn that his fate was to sail to Italy and there to establish a new home for his people.

Sailing westward, the Trojans stopped on one of a group of islands known as the Strophades. No sooner had they slaughtered some cattle, cooked the meat, and settled down for a meal, when a flock of Harpies descended on them and fouled the food. Aeneas and his followers managed to drive the creatures away. But the retreating Harpies uttered this combination of prophecy and curse: "You will make it to Italy, but you will not be allowed to establish a walled city of your own until hunger has driven you to de-vour your tables." (When Aeneas and his followers later sailed up the Tiber River in Italy, they stopped to eat and were so hungry that after finishing their meal they ate the thin bread-cakes they were using as platters; Aeneas interpreted these as their "tables" and concluded that the Harpies' prophecy had been fulfilled.)

Dido and Carthage

After the Harpies had departed, Aeneas continued westward, constantly harassed by the goddess Juno, who still harbored resentment toward the Trojans for her loss of the golden apple in the judgment of Paris. Eventually, the travelers reached the north African shore. There, Aeneas met Dido, a noblewoman from the Phoenician city of Tyre (in what is now Palestine in the eastern Mediterranean), who had recently fled her native land and was in the process of founding a new city—Carthage. Aeneas's mother, Venus, made Dido fall in love with her son, and for a while it looked as though the Trojan prince might forget about his prophesied Italian destiny and settle in Carthage. But eventually mighty Jupiter sent his messenger Mercury to remind Aeneas that he had a duty to future generations of Italians. Mercury asked Aeneas:

> Is it for you to lay the stones for Carthage's high walls . . . oblivious of your own world, your own kingdom? . . . If future history's glories do not affect you, if you will not strive for your own honor, think of Ascanius [Aeneas's son], think of the expectations of your heir, Julus [a later name for Ascanius, from whom the members of

the Roman Julii family, among them Julius Caesar, claimed descent], to whom the Italian realm, the land of Rome, are due.[44]

Hearing this appeal, Aeneas gave in and made preparations to leave Carthage. Dido was both grief stricken and angry that he would leave her this way, and despite her love for him, she pronounced a terrible curse. "May future Carthaginians and Aeneas's descendants always hate one another," she cried. "Let there be no treaties between the two peoples and let generation after generation be consumed by weapons and war!"[45]

Aeneas Learns of Rome's Destiny

After departing Africa, Aeneas sailed to Cumae in southern Italy. A prophet had earlier told him to seek out the Sibyl, a wise woman who could see into the future.

Urged on by Cupid, Aeneas (left) falls in love with Dido (right), ruler of Carthage.

The Mediterranean World

The Sibyl greeted him and told him that he was destined to fight a war in Italy over the right to marry an Italian bride. He then begged her to help him find a way into the underworld so that he might once more see his beloved father, who had died during the journey across the Mediterranean. Granting the request, the Sibyl led Aeneas down into the underworld, and in time they found the spirit of old Anchises.

After their reunion, the father offered to show the son the future of the grand and blessed race Aeneas would sire. "Come then," said Anchises, "I shall show you the whole span of our destiny." First, he revealed, Aeneas's offspring would found the city of Alba Longa in the Italian region of Latium; and the line of Alba's noble rulers would lead to Romulus, who himself would establish a city—none other than Rome.[46] "Under his tutelage," Anchises predicted, "our glorious Rome shall rule the whole wide world [and] her spirit shall match the spirit of the gods."[47] Anchises showed his son the long line of noble Romans, finally culminating in the greatest of them all, Augustus Caesar, who was destined to bring about a new golden age for Rome and humanity.[48]

After Aeneas and the Sibyl returned from their journey through the lower depths, the hero traveled northward to Latium to fulfill the destiny that had been revealed to him. He met the local ruler, Latinus, and soon sought the hand of that

How Romulus Gave His Name to Rome

The first-century B.C. *Roman historian Titus Livius, popularly known as Livy, wrote a huge history of Rome from its founding to his own time (142 books, 35 of which survive), in which he included some of the most popular Roman foundation myths. In this excerpt (translated by Aubrey de Sélincourt in* The Norton Book of Classical Literature*),* Romulus and Remus, descendants of Aeneas, quarrel over who will rule the new city.

"Romulus and Remus [after a successful struggle for recognition as rightful members of Alba Longa's royal house] . . . were suddenly seized by an urge to found a new settlement on the spot where they had been left to drown as infants and had been subsequently brought up. . . . Unhappily, the brothers' plans for the future were marred by . . . jealousy and ambition. A disgraceful quarrel arose from a matter in itself trivial. As the brothers were twins and all questions of seniority were therefore precluded, they determined to ask the gods of the countryside to declare by augury [omens, symbolic signs] which of them should govern the new town once it was founded, and give his name to it. . . . Remus, the story goes, was the first to receive a sign—six vultures; and no sooner was this made known to the people than double the number of birds appeared to Romulus. The followers of each promptly saluted their masters as king. . . . Angry words ensued, followed all too soon by blows, and in the course of the fray Remus was killed. There is another story, a commoner one, according to which Remus, by way of jeering at his brother, jumped over the half-built walls of the new settlement, whereupon Romulus killed him in a fit of rage, adding the threat, 'So perish whoever else shall overleap my battlements.' This, then, was how Romulus obtained the sole power. The newly built city was called by its founder's name."

king's daughter, Lavinia. But Turnus, prince of a neighboring people called the Rutulians, had already asked for Lavinia's hand, and the rivalry over Lavinia soon led to a terrible war, thus fulfilling the Sibyl's prophecy that Aeneas would fight over an Italian bride.

Eventually, Aeneas defeated Turnus and married Lavinia. From the union of the Trojan and Latin races, fulfilling the destiny ordained by Father Jupiter himself, sprang the lineage of the noble Romans, who would one day rule all the world. For the Romans, Jupiter had earlier told Venus, "I see no measure nor date [and] I grant them dominion without end . . . the master-race, the wearers of the Toga."[49]

Chapter

4 Triumphing over All Obstacles: Tales of Love and Lovers

That the Greeks and Romans had a strong romantic flair is evidenced by the large number of classical myths dealing with love and lovers. Even more revealing is the frequent development in these stories of perhaps the most romantically optimistic of all love themes—namely, that true love will triumph over all obstacles, no matter how daunting. For example, in one of the five following tales, that of Cupid and Psyche, a young maiden's love is able to withstand the formidable wrath of the goddess Venus; and in the story of Pygmalion and Galatea, romantic longing inspires the transformation of lifeless and loveless matter into completely responsive and loving flesh and blood. In fact, even death cannot part many mythical lovers, as shown so movingly in the tales of Baucis and Philemon and Pyramis and Thisbe.

That Ovid is the main source for so many of these myths about love seems fitting. He was the classical love poet par excellence, whose amorous collections—among them the *Art of Love*, the *Loves*, and the *Heroines*—were widely popular in his own time, as well as during the later European Renaissance. "Ah, hapless me," he wrote in the first section of his *Loves*, "Love's arrow did but all too surely find its mark. On fire am I, and Love, and none

but Love, now rules my heart that never was slave till now." [50]

Ovid did not invent the love myths he told, of course. Most had been part of common Greek and Roman folk heritage for centuries, and of these some had no doubt originated in neighboring foreign lands; for example, the tale of Pyramis and Thisbe came to Greece and then to Rome from Cilicia (in southern Asia Minor) or perhaps from ancient Babylonia (what is now Iraq), where the story is set. Of the following tales, all but that of Cupid and Psyche are from Ovid's *Metamorphoses*. The sole source of Cupid and Psyche is *The Golden Ass*, the only surviving complete Latin novel, by the second-century A.D. Roman writer Apuleius. [51] Whatever written sources Apuleius may have consulted for the various sections of the myth are now lost.

Cupid and Psyche

According to Apuleius, true love overcame Venus's anger in the following manner. A certain city was ruled by a king and queen who had three lovely daughters, the youngest of which, Psyche, was so strikingly beautiful that people journeyed

TRIUMPHING OVER ALL OBSTACLES: TALES OF LOVE AND LOVERS ■ **57**

A Not So Happy Ending

Not all of the myths about lovers have happy, reassuring, or nobly transcendent endings. Here, as summarized by Edith Hamilton in her famous retelling of the classic myths, is one of the tales in which the lovers end up neither together nor fulfilled. The main characters are Aurora, goddess of the dawn, and her husband Tithonus, one of the mortal sons of King Priam of Troy.

"Tithonus himself had a strange fate. Aurora asked Zeus to make him immortal and he agreed, but she had not thought to ask also that he should remain young. So it came to pass that he grew old, but could not die. Helpless at last, unable to move hand or foot, he prayed for death but there was no release for him. He must live on forever, with old age forever pressing upon him more and more. At last in pity the goddess laid him in a room and left him, shutting the door. There he babbled endlessly, words with no meaning.

His mind had gone with his strength of body. He was only the dry husk of a man. There is a story too that he shrank and shrank in size until at last Aurora, with a feeling for the natural fitness of things, turned him into the skinny and noisy grasshopper."

Aurora, also called Eos, daughter of the Titan Hyperion, rides her chariot through the sky, bringing the dawn.

from far and wide just to gaze at her. In fact, the local residents were so taken with the maiden that they began giving her wreaths and flowers when she walked through the streets. Soon they neglected their usual worship of the goddess Venus and started offering their prayers to Psyche instead.

It did not take long for Venus to see what was happening. Apuleius wrote:

> Since divine honors were being diverted in this excessive way to the worship of a mortal girl, the anger of the true Venus was fiercely kindled. She could not control her irritation. She tossed her head, let out a deep growl, and spoke. . . . "Here am I, the ancient mother of the universe . . . the Venus that tends the entire world, compelled to share the glory of my majesty with a mortal maiden, so that my name which has its niche in heaven is degraded by the foulness of the earth below! . . . This girl, whoever she is, is not going to enjoy appropriating the honors that are mine; I shall soon ensure that she rues the beauty which is not hers by rights![52]

The irate goddess summoned her handsome son, Cupid, and bade him help her exact her revenge on Psyche. Venus ordered Cupid to make the girl fall madly in love with the vilest, most despicable, most disreputable man on earth; that way her great beauty would be wasted and her life miserable.

At first, Cupid had every intention of helping his mother. But when he first

Cherubs flutter above, sea nymphs bear gifts, and Triton, Poseidon's son, blows his conch shell (at lower right) as the goddess Aphrodite rises from the waves.

caught sight of Psyche, his heart melted with love for her, almost as if he had been shot by one of his own love arrows. Thus the fate he arranged for the maiden was not exactly the kind Venus had intended. Time passed and Psyche's sisters each married wealthy kings; but strangely, no man asked to marry Psyche. Her parents became so confused and disturbed that they consulted an oracle of Apollo, not realizing that the god was cooperating in Cupid's scheme. Through the oracle, Apollo declared that the maiden would have to be dressed in black and left alone on a mountain, where a frightening winged serpent would descend and take her for its wife. Fearing to defy the god's will, Psyche's parents obeyed.

But once the girl was alone on the mountain, instead of a deadly serpent she found a pleasant valley, a placid stream, and a small but beautifully crafted palace. Upon entering, she found the building's interior lush with gold and silver trim, comfortable furnishings, and storerooms filled with gleaming jewels and other treasures. Then she heard a voice that seemed to float to her out of the thin air:

> Why, my lady, do you gaze open-mouthed at this parade of wealth? All these things are yours. So retire to your room, relieve your weariness on your bed, and take a bath at your leisure. . . . Once you have completed your toilet a royal feast will at once be laid before you.[53]

Psyche had not a clue about the identity of the voice's owner. But she was relieved that she had not been sacrificed to the serpent and therefore did what she was told and enjoyed a magnificent feast. That night, as she lay awake in bed, she felt someone climb into the bed with her. She could not tell who it was because the visitor was invisible in the dark, but she immediately recognized the voice she had heard earlier. The two entered into a tender and loving relationship, crowned by the invisible lover taking Psyche as his wife. All would be well, he said, as long as she made no attempt to try to see what he really looked like, and thereafter he spent night after night with her, each time departing swiftly just before the breaking of dawn.

Psyche's Unfortunate Mistakes

The lovers' happy relationship was interrupted, however, when Psyche's two sisters came to the mountain looking for her. Her husband warned her not to make contact with them, for they would only bring trouble; but she saw them crying, apparently over having lost her, and soon greeted them. When they seemed glad to see her alive, Psyche showed them the magnificent palace in which she had been living and eventually told them about her invisible husband.

Unbeknownst to Psyche, her sisters were consumed with jealousy about her palace, treasures, and marital bliss, all of which were far greater than their own, and they hatched a plan to bring her ruin and unhappiness. They convinced her that there was something sinister about the husband never showing himself and that he must in reality be the very hideous serpent of which Apollo's oracle had spoken. Psyche must destroy this deceptive creature, they advised. She must wait until it fell asleep, illuminate it with a lamp, and then stab it to death with a sharp razor.

Psyche became so afraid her sisters might be right that she decided to follow their advice. That night, her husband reclined on a comfortable couch and fell into a deep sleep. Gathering her courage, Apuleius wrote,

> she uncovered the lamp, seized the razor, and showed a boldness that belied her sex. But as soon as the lamp was brought near, and the secrets of the couch were revealed, she beheld of all beasts the gentlest and sweetest, Cupid himself, a handsome god lying in a handsome posture. Even the lamplight was cheered and brightened on sighting him. . . . As for Psyche, she was awe-struck at this wonderful vision, and she lost all of her self-control. She swooned and paled . . . [and] her knees buckled. . . . She gazed down on him in distraction, and as she passionately smothered him with wanton kisses from parted lips, she feared that he might stir in his sleep. But while her wounded heart pounded . . . the lamp disgorged a drop of burning oil . . . upon the god's right shoulder. . . . [He] started up on being burnt; he saw that he was exposed [to her sight], and that his trust was defiled. Without a word, he at once flew away from the kisses and embrace of his most unhappy wife.[54]

Realizing she had betrayed Cupid's trust, the distraught Psyche determined to find him and somehow to make it up to him, even if she had to search for the rest of her days. But when her efforts continually proved fruitless, in despair she decided to risk all and confront the goddess Venus and beg for her help. Having learned that her son had lavished wealth and love on this insolent mortal, Venus was angrier than ever. She proceeded to assign Psyche a series of tasks, claiming that if the girl completed them successfully she would help her; but Venus knew full well that the tasks were seemingly impossible for a mortal, so that the maiden was doomed to fail. To the goddess's surprise, however, Psyche (aided by various kindly woodland creatures) managed to complete the tasks.

It was then that Psyche made another unfortunate mistake. Venus had ordered her to carry a box into the underworld, to ask Dis's mate, Prosperina, to fill it with some of her beauty, and to bring the box back to Venus. Everything went smoothly until after the maiden, bearing the box, returned to the earth's surface. She could not resist the temptation to look inside, and when she did so Venus punished her by making her fall into a deep sleep. At last, the goddess felt as though she had exacted her revenge on the girl.

A Happy Ending

But not long afterward, Cupid intervened. Despite the earlier breach of trust, he still deeply loved Psyche and had been pining away for her. Finding her, he released her from the spell and then approached Father Jupiter, who agreed to help him. According to Apuleius, Jupiter gathered together all the gods, including Venus, and proclaimed:

> "You certainly all know this young man, whose impetuous youth, I believe, should be curbed by some kind of bridle. He has chosen a girl and

An Infernal Journey into the Underworld

In this excerpt from The Golden Ass, the Roman novelist Apuleius describes the advice given to Psyche by a tower that springs to life as she contemplates throwing herself from it. The tower tells the despairing girl how to make it safely to Prosperina in Dis's (Pluto's) underworld palace and thereby to accomplish the task given her by Venus. This episode probably began as a separate myth, which, along with others, became part of the larger story of Cupid and Psyche.

"The tower suddenly burst into speech and said: 'Listen to me. Sparta, the famed Greek city, lies not far from here. On its borders you must look for Taenarus, which lies hidden in a trackless region. Dis has his breathing vent there. . . . Once you have crossed the threshold . . . the track will lead you directly to [Dis's] palace. But you are not to advance through the dark region altogether empty-handed, but carry in both hands barley-cakes baked in sweet wine, and have between your lips twin coins. When you are well advanced on your infernal journey, you will meet a lame ass carrying a load of logs, with a driver likewise lame; he will ask you to hand him some sticks . . . but you must pass by in silence. . . . Immediately after that you will reach the lifeless river over which Charon [boatman of the dead] presides. . . . You must allow this squalid elder to take for your fare one of the coins . . . but he must remove it from your mouth with his own hand. Then . . . as you cross the sluggish stream, an old man now dead will float up to you, and raising his decaying hands will beg you to drag him into the boat; but you must not. . . . When you have crossed the river . . . some aged women weaving at the loom will beg you to lend a hand for a short time. But you are not permitted to touch that either. . . . Posted [outside Dis's abode] there is a massive hound with a huge, triple-formed head. . . . You must disarm him by offering him a cake as his spoils. Then you can easily pass him and gain immediate access to Prosperina herself. She will welcome you in a genial and kindly fashion, and she will try to induce you to sit on a cushioned seat beside her and enjoy a rich repast. But you must settle on the ground, ask for coarse bread, and eat it. Then you must tell her why you have come.'"

made her his wife. Let him keep her and possess her, and as he embraces Psyche may he always enjoy his love."

Then, turning his eyes toward Venus, Jupiter said, "And you, my daughter, must not be saddened at all nor have any fear because of this marriage with a mortal."[55]

Having said this, Jupiter ordered that Psyche be brought before the gods and given a cup of ambrosia, the magical liquid that would make her immortal and one of their number. By this means Venus's anger turned to delight, and the deep bond between Cupid, god of love, and Psyche, whose name means the soul, became unbreakable and eternal.

Pygmalion and Galatea

Venus figures prominently in another tale of seemingly impossible love—the story of Pygmalion, a gifted young sculptor. Pygmalion had convinced himself that women were weak, deceitful, and otherwise flawed by nature and that no matter how hard they tried they could not overcome this curse. So he determined never to marry and to live always alone.

In time, the young man began working on a statue of a lovely young woman, which was ironic considering how he detested the female gender. Perhaps he was trying to create the image of a hypothetically perfect woman in order to demonstrate what women might have been if they had not been endowed with so many faults. Whatever his motivation, as the work progressed, he devoted more and more of his time, patience, and genius to it, and the statue eventually took on the form of a maiden of radiant and matchless beauty.

So perfect was Pygmalion's creation that, against his will, he fell passionately in love with it. "The best art, they say," Ovid wrote, "is that which conceals art, and so

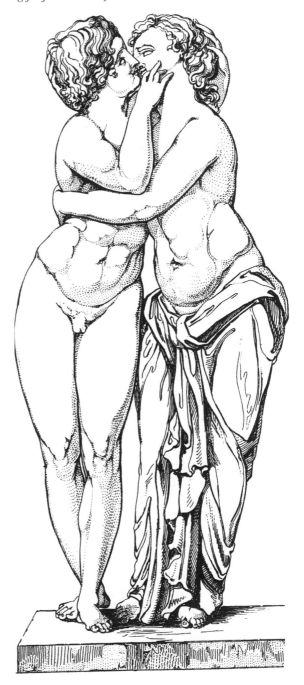

A drawing of a sculpture depicting the lovers Cupid and Psyche. Although Psyche began life as a mortal, because of Cupid's love for her the gods gave her the gift of immortality.

Pygmalion marveled, and loved the body he had fashioned." He would touch the unmoving ivory flesh, imagining in his mind's eye that it was real flesh, and the statue soon began to preoccupy much of his daily routine.

> He kissed, he fancied she returned; he spoke to her, held her, believed his fingers almost left an imprint in her limbs, and feared to bruise her. He paid her compliments, and brought her presents such as girls love, smooth pebbles, winding shells, little pet birds, flowers with a thousand colors, lilies, and painted balls, and lumps of amber. He decked her limbs with dresses, and her fingers wore rings which he put on, and he brought a necklace, and earrings, and a ribbon for her bosom . . . and took her to bed, put a soft pillow under her head, as if she felt it, [and] called her *Darling, my darling love!* [56]

This went on until the holiday commemorating Venus's famous birth from the sea foam. Like his neighbors, Pygmalion took part in the festival honoring the goddess, stood at one of her altars, burned incense, made a sacrificial offering, and prayed. He fervently beseeched Venus to help him find a wife that would be as perfect, blameless, and faultless as his ivory creation if, of course, such a woman actually existed, which he doubted. Luckily for the young artist, Venus heard his prayer and revealed her presence by making the altar flame jump three times.

Later in the day, Pygmalion went home. He approached the statue and caressed it, fully expecting the usual coldness and lack of response. But to his great surprise, the ivory flesh seemed warm. In a rising tide of excitement, he "wondered, and doubted, was dubious and happy, played lover again, and over and over touched the body with his hand. It *was* a body! The veins throbbed under the thumb." [57] Then what had once been a mere statue, but was now a living, breathing maiden, stared into his eyes, smiled, and returned his hugs. Pygmalion realized that this miracle had been Venus's work, and he thanked the goddess from the bottom of his heart. Venus was so pleased that she later attended the marriage between Pygmalion and the bride he had named Galatea. In time the lovers had a daughter named Paphos, who gave her name to the city that housed the goddess's most famous and beautiful temple.

Pomona and Vertumnus

Mortals like Psyche and Pygmalion were not the only ones who searched for and finally found perfect and lasting love. Take, for instance, the charming story of the only wood nymph who cared nothing for the woods—the beautiful Pomona. All that mattered to her, in fact, were her fruit-filled gardens and orchards, which she was careful to keep fenced off so that rustic country people, especially crude young men, could not trample her plants and vines.

Pomona also kept her orchards closed because she wanted to discourage the parade of young deities who, attracted to her good looks, regularly pursued her. These included many dancing satyrs, who looked like a cross between men and goats; Silenus, the important satyr who directly attended Bacchus, god of the vine; and Priapus, the fertility god who was known

Pomona, a minor Roman deity of gardens and orchards, contemplates some of the fruits and flowers that she supposedly spent all of her time tending.

for brandishing his sickle to frighten away thieves. The serious-minded nymph continually turned away all of these would-be lovers and husbands.

But then Vertumnus, the handsome young god of the changing seasons and patron of fruits, decided to try his hand at winning the reclusive Pomona. At first he came to her in various disguises, including a reaper, a vine pruner, an apple picker, a fisherman, and a soldier; but in each instance, although he was able to spend a few joyous moments gazing on her beauty, she paid him not the slightest attention. Finally, Vertumnus decided to try a different approach. He dressed himself as an old woman, gained entrance to Pomona's gardens, and pretended to admire her fruit. Saying that she was even more admirable than this very admirable crop, he startled her by kissing her on the mouth a good deal more intimately than any old woman would have.

Then the disguised god launched into a speech designed to arouse the nymph's interest in himself. He said, according to Ovid:

> A thousand men, although you shun and scorn them, still desire you. But if you will be wise [and] make a good match, pay heed to an old woman like me. . . . Reject those nobodies and choose Vertumnus to go to bed with. . . . I know him, if not better than he knows himself, at least as well. . . . He is different than the rest, he does not love the latest girl he sees. He is not fickle, you will be his first and last and only love all through his life, and he is young and charming. . . . [A]nd he loves the things that you do: he is always first to cherish the apples you love.[58]

Vertumnus further tried to sway Pomona by telling her the story of a hard-hearted young maiden who rejected a youth who loved her; in despair, the youth hanged himself, and Venus punished the girl by turning her to stone.

But none of Vertumnus's tricky speeches and stories had any effect on Pomona, and he realized that his disguise was worthless. Finally resigned that he would never win her, he tore off his old woman's garb and stood before her in all his godlike radiance. To his surprise and joy, the straightforward truth did the trick. When Pomona saw him, she was enchanted by his beauty, which was no less than her own, and from that day on they tended her gardens and orchards together.

Baucis and Philemon

By virtue of being deities, Pomona and Vertumnus had the benefit of forever appearing strong and youthful. Mortal lovers, on the other hand, inevitably grow old. Nevertheless, as the following story of how the oak and linden trees came to grow together demonstrates, human love has been known to remain steadfast in old age and even to transcend the dark curtain of death.

One of Jupiter's favorite pastimes was disguising himself as a mortal and roaming the earth in search of diversions and adventures. On one particular day, he and his messenger, Mercury, dressed themselves as lowly beggars and descended to the land of Phrygia (in central Asia Minor) to test the hospitality of the local people. To their dismay, the gods encountered much rudeness and selfishness. As

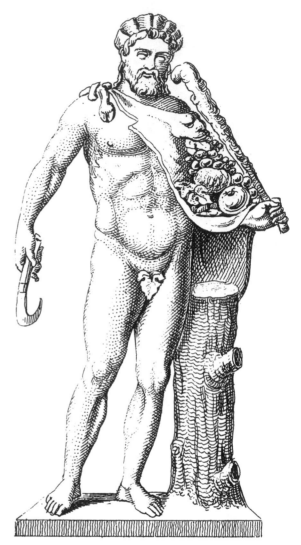

Vertumnus, the minor Roman god of the changing seasons and the divine patron of fruits.

they went from house to house, rich ones and poor ones alike, asking humbly for a scrap of food and a place to sleep, one owner after another told them to go away and barred the door against them. They tried a thousand houses and always received the same poor treatment.

Finally, Jupiter and Mercury came to a small hut thatched with straw and reeds, the humblest and poorest hovel they had seen so far. This time, an elderly couple, Baucis and Philemon by name, welcomed them in. As Ovid told it: They had married young and were deeply in love.

> They had grown old together in the same cottage; they were very poor, but faced their poverty with cheerful spirit and made its burden light by not complaining. It would do you little good to ask for servants or masters in that household, for the couple were all the house; both gave and followed orders.[59]

The two old people went out of their way to make the strangers comfortable. Baucis carefully washed her wobbly wooden table, and she and her husband prepared a supper of cabbage, olives, radishes, eggs, and whatever else edible they could find. As they and their guests ate the meal, Baucis and Philemon noticed that each time their mixing bowl was near to empty, it suddenly filled up again; and the wine kept on replenishing itself, too. Not realizing that this was the work of their superhuman guests, the two humans became afraid and raised their hands high in prayer.

At this moment, Jupiter and Mercury revealed themselves to the old people. They told them not to fear and led them to a mountaintop. From that vantage, Baucis and Philemon watched as a great flood drowned all their neighbors, the ones who had treated the gods so badly, a deluge that left only their own hut standing unscathed. Jupiter then transformed the hut into a magnificent temple, and the two mortals thereafter resided in it as his devoted priests.

The king of the gods did the two aging lovers a further kindness, ensuring that neither would have to endure the sadness and loneliness of outliving the other and also

Baucis and Philemon (right) do their best to entertain two wandering travelers, not realizing that their guests are really the powerful gods Jupiter and Mercury, who are on a mission to test the quality of human hospitality.

that they would remain together for eternity. On the last day of their lives each suddenly saw leaves sprouting from the other.

Philemon watched Baucis changing, Baucis watched Philemon, and as the foliage spread, they still had time to say "Farewell, my dear!" and the bark closed over sealing their mouths. And even to this day the peasants in that district show the stranger the two trees close together, and the union of oak and linden in one [trunk].[60]

Pyramis and Thisbe

As kindly Baucis and Philemon were joined inseparably in death, so too were a pair of lovers named Pyramis and Thisbe. These young people lived with their families in Babylon, where their two houses shared a common wall. Because they lived so close to each other, the boy and girl became well acquainted, and finally they fell in love. Naturally enough, they wanted to get married, but their parents, for reasons of their own, forbade it and tried to keep them apart.

Soon, however, Pyramis and Thisbe found a small hole in the wall that separated their houses, and through this opening they communicated their feelings for each other. Ovid told how they used to talk through the wall:

The loving whispers went back and forth in safety. They would stand one on each side, listening for each other, happy if each could hear the other's breathing, and then they would . . . say *Good-night!* and give the good-night kisses that never reached the other.[61]

Growing tired of having no other connection except this meager hole in the wall, Pyramis and Thisbe hatched a plan to escape from their parents and run away together. They agreed to meet at night near a tall mulberry tree covered with snow-white berries. When the sun went down, Thisbe slipped away from her house and made her way to the tree, where she saw that her lover had not yet arrived. While she was waiting for him, she suddenly spied a lioness approaching, its jaws covered with blood after a recent kill; and fearful that the beast might attack her too, she fled. But in her haste, she dropped her cloak. The curious lioness walked over, sniffed the garment, and then tore it to pieces before sauntering away into the night shadows.

A Tragic Turn of Events for the Young Lovers

Only seconds later, Pyramis arrived, expecting to meet his lovely Thisbe. But instead he found only the bloodstained remnants of the cloak, which he instantly recognized as hers. "It is all my fault!" he cried out, grief stricken. "I am the murderer, poor girl; I told you to come here in the night . . . and was not here to protect you. . . . Come, lions, all of you . . . drink my blood too!"[62] With these words, the distraught boy plunged a knife into his body and fell to the ground, while his blood spurted out over the white mulberries, staining them a deep red. Not long afterward, as he lay dying, Thisbe returned. Seeing the ghastly scene and her lover's hopeless condition, she decided to die with him, and after telling him that death

Dying for Love

The basic premise of the tale of Pyramis and Thisbe—separated lovers who attempt to get together but die in the process—is repeated in the myth of Hero and Leander, here retold by Max Herzberg in Myths and Their Meanings.

"On the Hellespont [the narrow strait that separates Greece from Asia Minor], almost directly opposite each other, lived a youth named Leander . . . and a maiden named Hero. . . . Hero's beauty was such that it was said that both Apollo and Cupid sued for her hand, but in vain. Now Hero served Venus as a priestess, and on a day it happened that Leander came [to the temple] . . . to do honor to the goddess. There he beheld Hero, and she at the same moment saw him, and both fell in love at first sight. But Hero's parents would not listen to the suit of Leander, and they even forbade the young people from seeing each other. Not so easily were they thwarted, however. They managed to arrange a code of signals, and whenever Hero at night hung a lantern upon the tower of the temple, Leander would swim the Hellespont and join her for a brief hour or two. But one night a storm arose after Leander had already set out on his dangerous journey. Shortly the winds blew out the guiding lantern, and Leander instead of swimming to safety directed his course toward a treacherous patch of sea. In vain he struggled; the storm was too much for him, and he perished. Next morning the waves washed his body ashore at the very feet of Hero. . . . In deep grief she threw herself into the ocean and was drowned."

In a fit of despair after finding the dead body of her lover, Hero hurls herself into the sea.

This exquisite ancient Roman painting of Pyramis and Thisbe was discovered in the summer dining room of the House of Tibertinus in Pompeii. The eruption of Mount Vesuvius in A.D. 79 buried the town in a layer of ash that preserved this and other art treasures.

would never keep them apart, she used the very same knife on herself. The two died together in the moonlight.

When Pyramis's and Thisbe's parents discovered what had happened, they were filled with shame and grief. They placed the lovers' ashes in one urn, where the boy's and girl's remains, mingling together, became eternally inseparable. The gods, their hearts filled with pity as they looked on from high above, created a lasting memorial for the unfortunate lovers, ordaining that thereafter the mulberry would bear only deep red fruit.

5 Cursed by the Gods: Divine Punishment for Human Folly

One of the most common themes in classical mythology was the wrath of the gods, brought down on humans for a variety of reasons. Sometimes the gods punished people for what were clearly direct affronts, or sins, committed against the divine personages. Athena's command that the Greek victors at Troy be punished for violating the sanctity of her temple and Jupiter's drowning of the Phrygian residents who had shown him inhospitality (in the tale of Baucis and Philemon) are well-known examples.

Two of the worst crimes committed by humans against the gods were those of Tantalus and Niobe. The gods saw Tantalus's acts as so despicable, in fact, that in addition to inflicting a dreadful punishment on him personally, they damned his family for generations, initiating the infamous curse of the House of Atreus (so named because Atreus was Tantalus's grandson). Compelled by the curse, some of Tantalus's descendants later committed heinous acts against their own relatives (for instance, Agamemnon's merciless sacrifice of his daughter Iphigenia prior to the Trojan War), perpetuating an awful cycle of hatred, violence, and human folly.[63]

On the other hand, at times humans in mythology suffered divinely inspired curses and retributions for much less serious and sometimes even seemingly innocent transgressions. For example, it was hardly Phineus's fault that Apollo had granted him the gift of prophecy (in the legend of the Argonauts), yet Zeus, feeling threatened, punished poor Phineus anyway. Likewise, the misfortunes and sufferings of Oedipus, king of Thebes, were not the result of a direct attack on the gods, but rather, developed out of his and his father's quite understandable attempts at self-preservation. The two men had the arrogant audacity to think they could escape the dire predictions of a divine oracle, and for this they ended up paying a terrible price. Oedipus learned the hard way that humans, even the most admirable ones, must not challenge the will of the gods.[64]

Death Too Lenient for Tantalus

What was Tantalus's horrendous crime against the gods and the severe retribution they inflicted on him and his descendants? Tantalus was a mortal son of Zeus and as a young man was so liked and respected by all of the gods that they allowed him regularly to dine with them in their banquet hall on Mount Olympus.

They even extended to him favors no other human enjoyed, such as letting him taste their mystical ambrosia and dropping in to dine with him in his palace on earth.

But for reasons that to this day no one can fathom, Tantalus horribly betrayed the kindness and trust the gods had extended to him. Perhaps he secretly hated them; or maybe he thought himself their better and wanted to show how easily he could deceive them. Whatever his motives, one day when the divinities had arrived at his palace for supper, he had his own son Pelops slain, boiled in a large pot, cut into pieces, and served to his guests. They would, he reasoned gleefully, indulge in one of the lowest and uncivilized of all practices—cannibalism—without even knowing it.

But Tantalus's assumption that he could so easily fool the gods was a serious miscalculation. When they saw and smelled the dish he had served them, they realized full well what it was and recoiled with a mixture of horror and seething anger. They could have killed Tantalus instantly, of course, but they felt a quick death was too lenient for so reprehensible a crime. Instead, they hurled him into the depths of Hades, where eons later, Odysseus, while on his famous ten-year journey, observed Tantalus's continuing and eternal punishment:

> The old man was standing in a pool of water which nearly reached his chin, and his thirst drove him to unceasing efforts; but he could never get a drop to drink. For whenever he stooped in his eagerness to lap the water, it disappeared. The pool was swallowed up, and all he saw at his feet was the dark earth, which some mysterious power had parched. Trees spread their foliage high over the pool and dangled fruits above his head—pear trees and pomegranates, apple-trees with their glossy burden, sweet figs and luxuriant olives. But whenever the old man tried to grasp them in his hands, the wind would toss them up toward the shadowy clouds.[65]

As for poor Pelops, the gods took pity on him and restored him to life. Unfortunately, one of them, perhaps Demeter, had in haste taken a tiny taste of the dreadful meal Tantalus had served, and the result was that when the young man was reassembled, one shoulder was missing; so the gods fashioned him a replacement shoulder made of the finest ivory.

Niobe's Tears

Pelops went on to have a happy and productive life.[66] But he was one of only a handful of his family members and descendants to do so, for the gods never got over the crime Tantalus had attempted to perpetrate. They cast a curse upon the family, and Pelops's sister Niobe was the first, after Tantalus, to suffer its dire consequences.

At first, Niobe seemed to enjoy a pleasant and productive life, helping her husband, Amphion, to rule ancient Thebes in peace and prosperity. She bore seven handsome, strong sons and seven beautiful, graceful daughters. But Niobe had inherited Tantalus's overbearing pride, and in time this dangerous emotion began to guide and distort her actions. One day she approached a temple where some Theban women were praying and sacrificing to

The gods attempt to put poor Pelops back together after foiling Tantalus's grisly plot. But alas, a missing shoulder makes reassembling one arm difficult.

Leto, the Titan, mother of the gods Apollo and Artemis. She asked them:

> Why do you bother worshipping Leto when I myself am more worthy of such worship? Think about it. I'm just as beautiful as any goddess; and besides, I have fourteen wonderful children, while poor Leto has only two. Come, forget about Leto and lavish your attentions on me instead.

Leto soon found out about this grave insult to herself and her divine children.

The goddess immediately went to Apollo and Artemis and asked them to help her exact a suitable punishment, and they just as quickly agreed. They sped down from towering Olympus to Thebes and, in a savage bloodbath, used their mighty bows and arrows to slay all of Niobe's noble sons before her very eyes. The gods might have been satisfied with this load of vengeance had not Niobe continued to defy them. As Ovid told it:

> Niobe bent over the bodies of her sons, now cold in death, showering

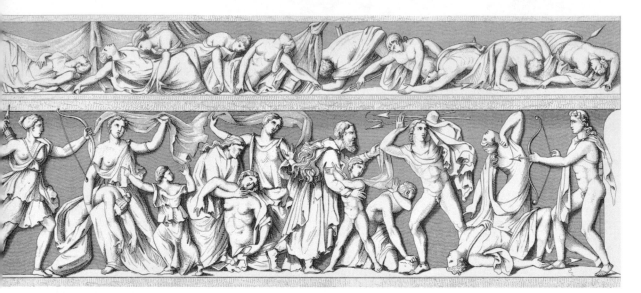

In the ancient frieze here depicted, some of Niobe's children lie slain by the arrows of the vengeful Apollo and Artemis (top), while the slaughter continues (below).

them in kisses. Then, raising her arms toward the heavens, she cried, "Feed, cruel Leto, on my grief. . . . Even in my misery I have more left to me than you have in your glory. Even after so many deaths I am the victor!" As she spoke the twang of the bowstring rang out, bringing terror. The sisters [Niobe's seven daughters] . . . were standing where their brothers lay in death. One as she pulled the arrow from his flesh, fell dying as she tried to kiss her brother's lips. A second, endeavoring to console her mother . . . suddenly fell silent and doubled up with a hidden wound. One sank down as she tried in vain to escape; another fell dead upon her sister. . . . When six had been taken by death, suffering various sorts of wounds, only one remained alive. Then the mother, shielding this last child with her body . . . cried out, "Leave this one for me . . . I pray you,

leave the smallest, leave one!" But even as she prayed, the one she prayed to save fell dead.[67]

Struck dumb with overpowering grief at the merciless slaughter of all her children, Niobe burst into tears. Even as she did so, she steadily solidified into stone, her final punishment from the divinities she had offended. Thereafter, both night and day, tears continued to spring from the stone and kept its surface moist, a warning to all who might contemplate insolence against the gods.

The Curse Passes to New Generations

The family curse next fell on Pelops's two sons, Thyestes and Atreus, who, through their own terrible deeds, passed it along to the succeeding generation. Thyestes fell in love with his brother's wife and had sexual relations with her behind Atreus's back. On learning of the affair, the enraged Atreus, taking inspiration from his grandfather Tantalus, killed Thyestes' two small children, cut them up, boiled them, and served them to their unsuspecting father. Because Atreus was king and had all the power, the distraught Thyestes could not retaliate and the crime went unavenged.

To be more precise, the crime was unavenged in Atreus's lifetime; however, dire retribution came to one of Atreus's offspring. His son Menelaus, ruler of Sparta and husband of Helen (whose flight with Paris had instigated the Trojan War), lived a reasonably uneventful and happy life once back in Greece after the fall of Troy. Thus the family curse skipped over Menelaus and fell with full force on Atreus's other son— Agamemnon, king of Mycenae.

Agamemnon's Murder

After leading the Greeks to victory at Troy and then surviving the storm sent by Poseidon to punish Greek sacrilege during the city's fall, Agamemnon returned to Mycenae in triumph. Huge crowds greeted the conquering hero as he disembarked his ship on the coast and accompanied him as he made his way across the fertile plain to his magnificent fortress-palace. To the king, all seemed festive and hopeful. But in the crowd were elder Mycenaeans who remembered with foreboding what had occurred before Agamemnon had departed for Troy. They recalled his brutal slaughter of his daughter Iphigenia and worried that this deed might be part of the continuing cycle of evil that was rumored to hang over the royal house of Atreus. Edith Hamilton writes:

Ten years had passed since Iphigenia died, but the results of her death reached through to the present. The elders were wise. They had learned that every sin causes fresh sin; every wrong brings another in its train. A menace from the dead girl hung over her father in this hour of triumph. And yet perhaps, they said to each other, perhaps it would not take actual shape for a time. So they tried to find some bit of hope, but at the bottom of their hearts they knew and dared not say aloud that vengeance was already there in the palace waiting for Agamemnon.[68]

Indeed, waiting inside was Agamemnon's wife, Clytemnestra, who had all these long years harbored deep-seated hatred and resentment toward him for the death of their innocent daughter. In the king's absence, she had taken a lover, Aegisthus, the youngest son of Thyestes (born after Thyestes had devoured his other sons); and now, with Aegisthus to help her, she put her plan for revenge into action. The elders who had gathered outside the palace heard Agamemnon's death cries, and only minutes later the queen appeared, her gown spattered with fresh blood, the dripping knife still in her hand. In his play *Agamemnon*, Aeschylus had her say:

I struck him twice. In two great cries of agony he buckled at the knees and fell. When he was down I struck him a third blow. . . . Thus he went down, and the life struggled out of him; and as he died he spattered me with the dark red and violent driven rain of bitter savored blood. . . . For me, I glory. Were it religion to pour wine above the slain, this man deserved, more than deserved, such sacrament. He filled our [family's] cup with things unspeakable and now himself come home has drunk it to the dregs.[69]

Orestes' Revenge

Clytemnestra and Aegisthus felt no guilt for what they had done, just as Agamem-non, Atreus, Niobe, and Tantalus had felt no guilt for their crimes; and because only guilt and suffering could cleanse the stains of such terrible acts, they, in their self-righteousness, inadvertently allowed the curse to continue to still another generation. Clytemnestra and Aegisthus ruled for many years, thinking that all was finally well in their land. But two of Agamem-non's children—his son Orestes and his daughter Electra—were still living. The young man grew up in a foreign land, safe from his mother and stepfather, who feared him and would surely have killed him if they had the chance. Electra grew up in the palace, miserable at having to live with her father's murderers, and

Aegisthus urges Clytemnestra to murder Agamemnon (visible in the background). Aeschylus's play Agamem-non *dramatizes the bloody crime, part of the continuing curse on the unfortunate House of Atreus.*

The vengeful Orestes was fated to carry on his family's crippling curse. This engraving of Orestes is based on the famous statue carved by the nineteenth-century Danish sculptor Hermann Bissen.

dreamed of the day when her brother might return home and exact vengeance.

That day finally came. Orestes, now fully grown and aching to avenge his father's murder, slipped into the palace and revealed himself to Electra. Together they plotted to kill Clytemnestra and Aegisthus, and Orestes actually executed these bloody deeds. But as he stood on the palace steps, the gore-spattered bodies sprawled behind him, he beheld some-thing terrifying that no others present could see—the snake-haired Furies, the tormentors of murderers, who had come to haunt and pursue him. He realized that, having perpetuated the awful family curse, he could not stay to sit on the throne that was rightfully his. According to Aeschylus, Orestes cried out:

I go, an outcast wanderer from this land, and leave behind, in life, in death, the name of what I did. . . . [The

Furies] come like gorgons [hideous women with snakes for hair], they wear robes of black, and they are wreathed in a tangle of snakes. I can no longer stay. . . . These are . . . the bloodhounds of my mother's hate. . . . Ah, Lord Apollo, how they grow and multiply, repulsive for the blood drops of their dripping eyes. . . . You cannot see them, but I see them. I am driven from this place. I can stay here no longer.[70]

Orestes wandered through many lands, always pursued by the fearsome Furies. Finally, having long felt great guilt for his acts, he journeyed to the temple of Athena in Athens and there asked the goddess for guidance and the purification of his sins. The wise Athena saw how Orestes was the first of the long line of killers in his family to suffer from his guilt, to seek absolution from the gods, and to throw himself on their mercy. So she accepted his plea. In this healing atmosphere of mercy and forgiveness, a wondrous thing happened: Athena transformed the hideous and vengeful Furies into the kindly and graceful Eumenides, protectors of all who beseech the gods. From that day forward, none of Orestes' descendants were doomed to perpetuate the sins of the past, for the destructive curse that had hung so long over the House of Atreus was at last extinguished.

Oedipus and the Sphinx

Horrible crimes, suffering, and guilt are also integral to the story of Laius and Oedipus, although their initial offenses against the gods were seemingly mild by comparison with those of Tantalus and Niobe. Laius was king of Thebes and the great-grandson of Cadmus, the man who had founded the city. Not long after Laius had married his distant cousin Jocasta, he consulted the Delphic oracle, which told him that he and his new wife would have a son but that Laius himself would one day die by that son's hand.

At the time, people commonly believed that Apollo's oracle never lied and that trying to subvert one of its prophecies was both futile and an expression of distrust for the god. But Laius, understandably fearful for his life, became determined to change the fate that had been decreed for him. When Jocasta bore him a son, he had the infant's feet bound together and ordered a servant to leave the child on the side of a mountain, where it would surely die. Confident that he had cheated fate, Laius breathed a sigh of relief and concentrated on ruling Thebes.

Many uneventful years passed. Then the people of Thebes suddenly found themselves beset by a serious crisis. A frightening monster began stalking the countryside around the city, a creature called the Sphinx, which had the body of a winged lion and the face of a human woman. The Sphinx would leap out at travelers and pose them a riddle; if a person could solve the riddle, the beast promised, it would let him or her go; if not, the Sphinx devoured the person alive. Because no one could solve the riddle, one Theban after another met doom in the creature's clutches and terror gripped the city. Making matters worse, news came that King Laius, now an old man, had been killed by robbers while traveling with some attendants along a road near Delphi. The widowed Jocasta

Clytemnestra's Last Moments

Having slain Aegisthus, Orestes confronted his mother, Clytemnestra. In this dramatic scene from Aeschylus's Libation Bearers *(Paul Roche's translation), mother and son exchange words before he kills her as well.*

ORESTES: You're the one I'm looking for. *This* wretch [the dead Aegisthus] has had enough.

CLYTEMNESTRA: Oh, no! Aegisthus dead? . . .

Orestes: You love that man? Then in the same grave with him you'll lie: faithful unto death and ever afterwards.

CLYTEMNESTRA: Wait, son, wait. My baby, soften toward this bosom where so many times you went to sleep. . . . I reared you up from babyhood. Oh, let me then grow old with you.

ORESTES: What! Slay my father—then come sharing homes with me?

CLYTEMNESTRA: Fate, my son, is half to blame for that.

ORESTES: Then Fate arranges for your dying now.

CLYTEMNESTRA: Son, does a parent's curse mean nothing to you?

ORESTES: Not a thing. You gave me birth, then flung me out—to misery. . . .

CLYTEMNESTRA: Your heart, it seems, my son, is set on murdering a mother.

ORESTES: You are the one, not I who does the murdering.

CLYTEMNESTRA: Watch, then, for a mother's curse: it will hound you down.

ORESTES: Or a father's if I let this go.

CLYTEMNESTRA: Am I crying my life away upon a tomb?

ORESTES: Yes, my father's fate is beckoning yours.

CLYTEMNESTRA: So *you* are the snake I bore and gave my breast to?

ORESTES: Yes. Your nightmare saw things straight. You killed a man you never should, now suffer what you never would.

and all of her subjects prayed to be delivered from their misery.

Their prayers seemed answered when a stalwart and intelligent young man named Oedipus, a traveler from the city of Corinth, appeared on the scene. He courageously confronted the monster, which naturally demanded that he solve the riddle. According to the first-century B.C. Greek historian Diodorus:

> This is what was set forth by the Sphinx: "What is it that is of itself two-footed, three-footed, and four-footed?" Although the others could not see through it, Oedipus replied that the answer was "man," for as an infant man begins to move as a four-footed being [crawling on all fours], when he

is grown he is two-footed, and as an old man he is three-footed, leaning upon a staff because of his weakness.[71]

Distraught over having been vanquished by a mere human, the Sphinx committed suicide. Thebes was saved, and the grateful citizens welcomed Oedipus as their king. He married Jocasta, had two sons with her, and many years of happiness and prosperity followed.

"I Shall Leave No Stone Unturned"

Eventually, however, the Thebans once more found themselves in a state of crisis.

This well-known illustration of Oedipus confronting the winged Sphinx was painted on an Athenian "red-figure" wine cup by the so-called Oedipus Painter, who worked in the fifth century B.C.

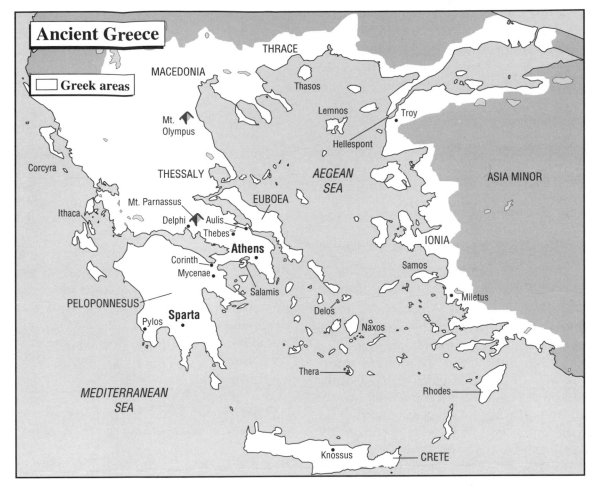

Ancient Greece

Greek areas

THRACE

MACEDONIA

Thasos

Lemnos

Troy

Mt. Olympus

Hellespont

Corcyra

THESSALY

AEGEAN SEA

ASIA MINOR

Mt. Parnassus

EUBOEA

Ithaca

Delphi   Aulis

Thebes

Athens

IONIA

Corinth

Samos

Mycenae

Salamis

Miletus

PELOPONNESUS

Delos

Pylos   Sparta

Naxos

MEDITERRANEAN SEA

Thera

Rhodes

Knossos   CRETE

A terrible plague fell upon the land, a blight that killed plants, livestock, and people alike. Determined to help his people, Oedipus sent his brother-in-law Creon to Delphi to consult the oracle; surely, they reasoned, the healing god Apollo would offer some saving piece of advice for the ailing city. And sure enough, Creon returned from Delphi with good news. The oracle had proclaimed that the plague would be lifted if and when the murderer of the former king, Laius, was apprehended and punished. Oedipus took up this cause enthusiastically. In the play *Oedipus the King*, Sophocles had him

say: "[I] will lend my support to avenging this crime against this land and the god as well. . . . I shall leave no stone unturned, for we shall succeed with the help of the god or be destroyed if we fail."[72]

But in his search for Laius's killer, Oedipus soon discovered some odd and disturbing information. First, the highly revered blind prophet Teiresias told him that he, Oedipus, was the very culprit for whom he searched. Teiresias declared:

You are the murderer. . . . *You* are the unholy defilement of this land. . . . You are a pitiful figure. . . . You, who have eyes, cannot see the evil in which you stand. . . . Do you even know who your parents are? Without knowing it, you are the enemy of your own flesh and blood, the dead below and the living here above. The double edged curse of your mother and father . . . shall one day drive you from this land. You see straight now but then you will see darkness. You will scream aloud on that day. . . . There is no man alive whose ruin will be more pitiful than yours.[73]

Sealing Their Own Fates

At first, Oedipus angrily dismissed these words, thinking it ridiculous that he could be the killer. Jocasta also rejected this idea. She explained to Oedipus that Laius had been murdered by robbers where three roads come together near Delphi; therefore, Oedipus was obviously not the guilty party. But hearing her describe the specific location of the crime made Oedipus suddenly perk up. "When exactly did this happen?" he asked his wife. "Why, just before you arrived in Thebes," she answered casually.

Increasingly worried and uneasy, Oedipus proceeded to tell Jocasta about how he had come to Thebes in the first place. He had been the loving son of Corinth's king and queen, Polybus and Merope. Upon learning from the Delphic oracle that he was fated to kill his own father and marry his own mother, the horrified Ocdipus had attempted to escape the prophecy by fleeing Corinth. If he never saw Polybus and Merope again, he reasoned, he could never end up killing one and marrying the other. Oedipus struck out for Thebes and in time, he told Jocasta:

I came near to [a] triple crossroads and there I was met by a herald and a man riding on a horse-drawn wagon, just as you described it. The driver, and the old man himself, tried to push me off the road. In anger, I struck the driver. . . . When the old man saw me coming . . . he aimed at my head . . . and hit me. I paid him back in full. . . . I killed the whole lot of them.[74]

As Oedipus and Jocasta continued to talk, a messenger arrived from Corinth, bringing them the news that old King Polybus had recently died. At first, it seemed as though this proved that the oracle's pronouncements could indeed be false or avoided. After all, Polybus was dead, and it was clear to all that Oedipus had had no hand in the deed, as the oracle had predicted he would.

Oedipus's Fall into Despair

But then the Corinthian messenger stepped forward and told a story that made Oedipus shudder and Jocasta turn pale. Oedipus was not Polybus's son, said the messenger; Polybus and Merope had brought him up as their own after he, the messenger, had presented him to them. And where had he gotten the child? A servant of the Theban king had secretly given him the baby.

Only minutes later, that very same servant, now an old man, confirmed the messenger's story. When Laius had ordered him to leave the baby outside to die, the servant had taken pity on it and given the baby to the Corinthian for safekeeping. The horrendous truth was now plain.

The Gods Take Oedipus

Oedipus's blinding and fall from power, dramatized by Sophocles in Oedipus the King, *did not mark the end of the former king's story. In Sophocles' last play,* Oedipus at Colonus, *composed in 406 B.C., the playwright told how the gods, seeing how long and hard Oedipus had suffered, finally forgave him. Historian Michael Grant (in* The Classical Greeks) *summarizes this beautiful and mysterious play.*

"The story is a sequel of *Oedipus the King*, at the end of which he had blinded himself and departed from Thebes. Now a ragged beggar, after years of wandering from place to place, he arrives at Colonus, near Athens, led by his daughter Antigone. The elders of Colonus, the chorus of the play, go to see him but are horror-struck when they learn who he is, and order him to leave . . . [however] King Theseus promises to help him, and frustrates Creon, who has arrived from Thebes to seize both the blind former monarch and Antigone (her sister Ismene has already been captured). . . . Thunderclaps tell Oedipus that his hour has come, and attended by Theseus and his daughters he leads the way to a place where he will depart from the land of the living. Halfway he bids Antigone and Ismene farewell, and what happened next no one but Theseus knew; but, according to a messenger's report, Oedipus was taken by the gods. Their justice has the last word; but we are not in a position to understand how it works. . . . The story of *Oedipus the King* has been modified, so that now he can declare that he is sinned against and not sinning: his tragic suffering justified and made meaningful by nobility of character, he has moved onwards from utter isolation to ultimate divine acceptance."

Oedipus, former king of Thebes, tenderly holds his daughter Antigone before he is taken by the gods.

Oedipus was indeed, as Teiresias had earlier claimed, the guilty man who had brought the curse of the gods down on Thebes. Both Laius and Oedipus had tried to escape their fates and in so doing had sealed them. The prophecy that Laius would die by his own son's hand had been fulfilled, and the oracular prediction that Oedipus would murder his father and marry his mother had also come to pass.

Soon Teiresias's own predictions, namely, that Oedipus would scream aloud and see darkness, came true as well. Unable to cope with the horror of his acts, the Theban king wailed like a mortally wounded animal and in a fit of despair gouged out his own eyes. As for Jocasta, the realization that she had married her own son and had children by him was too much for her, and she killed herself.

In this way, all involved learned the lesson that what the gods and fates decree no human can or should challenge. Oedipus's fall from the heights of prosperity and happiness to the depths of wretchedness and despair illustrated another lesson—that suffering is an inevitable part of life and takes the ultimate measure of every person, rich or poor, mighty or humble. As Sophocles put it in the conclusion of his great tragedy:

> O citizens of our native Thebes, behold: Here is Oedipus, who solved the renowned riddle and became ruler of our city and was regarded with envy by every citizen because of his good fortune. Think of the flood of terrible disaster that has swept over him. Thus, since we are all mortal, consider even a man's final day on earth and do not pronounce him happy until he has crossed the finish line of life without the pain of suffering.[75]

6 Mining an Ancient Legacy: The Classical Myths in Popular Culture

The classical myths and the characters who populated them were integral components of the religions of the early Greeks and Romans; and therefore these stories had a measurable influence and impact on most people's lives. Over time, as cultural attitudes changed, and especially later as Christianity became the principal religion of Western societies, the religious impact of the myths disappeared. Yet over the centuries they survived in many nonreligious forms and guises and steadily became absorbed into the folklore, literature, art, and music of the European-based nations that grew upon the wreckage of the old Greco-Roman world. Today, the events, themes, and characters of classical mythology remain vibrantly alive as new generations of writers, composers, and other artists, including filmmakers, continue to mine this rich ancient legacy.

Changing Views of Traditional Myths

The key factor in the survival of the classical myths was the fact that they were never rejected, thrown out, or substantially changed in content; instead, what changed was the way people viewed, interpreted, and accepted these stories. As early as the sixth century B.C., Greek scientists had begun to question traditional views of the universe, its structure, and humanity's place in nature. With the renaissance of Greek education and philosophy in the fifth and fourth centuries B.C., literal belief in the truth of the old myths weakened considerably, at least among scholars and well-educated people.[76] Many (although certainly not all) of the Greek myths, especially the more fantastic ones featuring monsters, journeys to the underworld, and the like, came to be regarded by many as little more than quaint folklore.

The religious truth of the classical myths received an even more serious blow after the fourth-century B.C. Greek conqueror Alexander the Great carved out a gigantic empire stretching from the Aegean sphere to the borders of ancient India. Alexander's campaigns significantly widened the cultural scope of the Greek world (and the Roman world that later absorbed it) by bringing the West into contact with eastern ideas, customs, and religions. The following two centuries or so, referred to as the Hellenistic Age, witnessed a tremendous outburst of cultural diversity and experimentation in numerous areas, including religion. Once again, the traditional Greek myths were not thrown out, but they were taken less seriously by those Greeks who turned for consolation to eastern religions.[77]

Although classical mythology remained very popular in Hellenistic times, interest in it was in large degree literary in nature. Greek writers working in what had become the Mediterranean world's intellectual center of Alexandria, Egypt—men like Callimachus and Apollonius of Rhodes—reveled in producing long works based or modeled on the traditional myths. Apollonius's widely popular epic, the *Argonautica*, was a typical example. But this so-called Alexandrian literature was created primarily for its entertainment value rather than for religious edification. It is revealing that the Alexandrian writers strongly influenced and inspired Ovid. Composing his *Metamorphoses* two centuries after their heyday, he lovingly retold the Greco-Roman myths; but plainly, he personally believed that few, if any, of them actually happened.

Explanation and Criticism

Another aspect of the Alexandrians' prodigious output ended up having an important effect on the way the classical myths were transmitted to the medieval and modern worlds. Callimachus and his colleagues were particularly fond of explaining the myths, often offering what seemed like logical theories for their origins. In particular, Euhemerus of Messene proposed that the Greek gods were originally human rulers and military heroes, who, over the course of time, had come to be seen as more powerful and exalted than they really had been. The Romans trans-

lated Euhemerus's writings into Latin; and later, when Christianity gained prominence in Rome, Christian writers used what had come to be called "Euhemerism" to attack the pagan (non-Christian) gods. In the fourth century A.D., Augustine (later made a saint), for instance, declared in his *City of God:*

> A far more credible account of these gods is given, when it is said that they were men, and that to each one of them sacred rites and solemnities were instituted, according to his particular genius, manners, actions, circumstances . . . the poets adorning them with lies, and false spirits seducing

A cameo of Publius Ovidius Naso (43 B.C.–ca. A.D. 17), popularly known as Ovid. His chief work, the Metamorphoses, *is the most famous and influential compendium of Greek and Roman myths ever written.*

Augustine of Hippo hands prayer books to Christian monks. His work, City of God, *denied the reality of the pagan gods.*

men to receive them. For it far more likely that some youth . . . being desirous to reign, dethroned his father, than that . . . Saturn was overthrown by his son, Jupiter.[78]

Yet, though Christian writers such as Augustine tried to trivialize the old gods and myths, they did not succeed in eliminating their prevalence and popularity. Christianity became Rome's official religion in the late fourth century A.D., when Augustine was a young man, and worship of the old gods was banned; but many Romans and Greeks remained pagans and carried on their rituals privately. By this time, very few such worshipers thought there was any truth to most myths, and these stories no longer had much real religious significance. But as long as the old faith survived, many people held them near and dear as symbols of their proud traditional past (similar to how many devout modern Christians look on the stories of Adam and Eve and Noah and the Ark as charming parts of their religious folklore rather than as literal fact).

The classical myths also retained their popularity in the belief system of astrology, which associated various stars, constellations, and planets with mythological names and subjects.[79] For example, the constellation now called Gemini, the Twins, then known as the Dioscuri, was thought to depict the brothers Castor and Pollux, who sailed with Jason on the *Argo.* And the ancients saw the star group today known as Cancer as a depiction of the crab said to have bitten the hero Hercules on the foot while he was attempting to kill a monstrous serpent.

The Myths Are Perpetuated

Meanwhile, as Rome fell in the fifth century A.D. and gave way to the kingdoms of medieval Europe, Christian writers often used the old pagan myths as examples (negative ones at first) when trying to teach moral lessons. In this manner, Christianity absorbed and perpetuated, rather than eliminated, these ancient tales. Morford and Lenardon explain:

> The [Christian] critics of classical mythology . . . actually assisted in the process of keeping it alive; the myths survived not only in classical literary texts (most especially the works of Virgil), but also in the religious tradition, where they were used by the Christians and can claim even to have enriched the religion that sought to destroy them. This process of absorption and mingling throughout the Middle Ages finds its ultimate medieval synthesis in the work of [the renowned thirteenth-century Italian poet] Dante, where the classical myths are used and criticized and, in the process, vindicated.[80]

A Rich Source of Literary References

Indeed, later medieval writers like Dante were both fascinated by and steeped in the classical myths. In large degree, this development stemmed initially from a huge resurgence of interest in Ovid's *Metamorphoses* during the eleventh, twelfth, and thirteenth centuries. As some of their predecessors had, Christian writers of this era used Ovid's tales as sources of allegory in which events, ideas, and characters became symbols illustrating moral lessons. The culmination of this fervid reworking of Ovid was the *Ovide Moralisé*, a fulsome fourteenth-century French version of the

Dante Alighieri (1265–1321). His Divine Comedy *(begun ca. 1307) depicts an imaginary journey through Hell, guided part of the way by the Roman mythologist Virgil.*

Metamorphoses rewritten to emphasize Christian morality.

As time went on, Dante and other great writers, including the sixteenth-century English playwright William Shakespeare and the seventeenth-century English poet John Milton, used Ovid's version of the classical myths as a rich source of literary allusions and references. Michael Grant comments:

> By his imaginative, inexhaustible store of word-pictures, Ovid became the master and model of Renaissance poets . . . and of the Elizabethan Age [sixteenth-century in England]. The *Metamorphoses* were famous in the

translation of [Elizabethan writer] Arthur Golding. . . . From his version came the mythological allusions with which Shakespeare abounds, and Milton's many detailed echoes.[81]

Merely listing Milton's references to mythology would consume dozens of pages; suffice it to say that his short poem *Comus* contains more than thirty such allusions and his epic poem *Paradise Lost* (published in 1667), hundreds.

As for Shakespeare, entire volumes have been written about his uses of classical mythology, which number in the thousands. He took some of these references directly from Ovid, Virgil, and other storehouses of myths; for example, in one of the most famous speeches in *Hamlet*, the title character compares his mother's crying after her husband's death to Niobe's tears after she has been turned to stone by Apollo and Artemis.[82] In that same speech, Hamlet also refers to the Greek sun god Hyperion, a goatlike satyr, and to the hero Hercules.

Other Shakespearean mythological connections are more indirect. The famous play *Romeo and Juliet*, written in the 1590s, is a case in point. The direct source of the play's story was English poet Arthur Brooke's 1562 poem, *The Tragical History of Romeus and Juliet*. Working backward, Brooke's work was based on a French translation of a story in Italian writer Matteo Bandello's 1554 work, *Novelle*; Bandello's inspiration appears to have been works by the earlier Italian writers Masuccio Salernitano and Luigi da Porto; and it is likely that these writers were, in their turn, influenced, at least in part, by the Greek myth of Pyramis and Thisbe, as told by Ovid.[83]

Shakespeare and his predecessors also made frequent use of the mythology surrounding the Trojan War. In his play *Troilus and Cressida*, Shakespeare depicted the love of King Priam's youngest son, Troilus, for a Trojan maiden during the eighth year of the siege of Troy. One of the major sources for the play was English writer Geoffrey Chaucer's lengthy 1380 poem, *Troilus and Criseyde*; and Chaucer's version was partly based on the *Roman de Troie*, or *Romance of Troy*, a thirty-thousand-line work composed by the French writer Benoît de Sainte-Maure in 1160, which included the exploits of the Argonauts and Odysseus as well as the events of the Trojan expedition.

Myths in Modern Literature

Modern literature is no less replete with references to the Trojan War and other ancient myths. Nineteenth-century American writer Edgar Allan Poe's poem "To Helen," a tribute to the beauty of the face that launched a thousand ships, is a well-known example. "On desperate seas long wont to roam," Poe wrote in part, "Thy hyacinth hair, thy classic face, thy Naiad [nymphlike] airs have brought me home to the glory that was Greece, and the grandeur that was Rome."[84]

In the twentieth century, an outstanding example is Irishman James Joyce's acclaimed novel *Ulysses*. This complex commentary on the state of modern society follows the main character, Leopold Bloom, in his journeys through Dublin, which, episode for episode, mirror the wanderings of the hero in Homer's *Odyssey*. Also noteworthy is American playwright Eugene O'Neill's *Mourning Becomes Electra*, a trilogy of dramas that retells the murderous saga of the House of Atreus in a post–Civil War New England setting.

Painters and Composers Interpret the Classical Myths

In the same way that they inspired playwrights, poets, and novelists, the classical myths also became rich sources of material for artists. Of the mythological paintings by the early great masters, one of the most famous is *The Birth of Venus*, by the fifteenth-century Italian Sandro Botticelli. This universally recognized work depicts the nude goddess standing in a huge clamshell, having just risen from the sea foam. Some of Botticelli's Italian contemporaries who also utilized mythological themes in their paintings included Bellini, Giorgione, and Titian.

Two other artists who earned notoriety for their depiction of mythical characters and scenes were Germany's Albrecht Dürer in the late 1400s and early 1500s and the seventeenth-century Flemish master Peter Paul Rubens. One of Dürer's most famous creations is the *Sky-Map of the Northern Hemisphere*, completed in 1515. The work shows a large circle representing the celestial sphere on which the major constellations appear in the mythical forms given them in classical times. Among others, the hero Hercules wields his club and lion skin; Perseus, another famous hero, holds the head of the snake-haired gorgon Medusa, whom he has just

Odysseus Still Calls the Commands

One of the many modern literary works inspired by classical mythology is the well-known poem "The Argonauts," by the English writer D. H. Lawrence (1885–1930), capturing Western society's continuing enchantment with the Mediterranean's ancient waterways.

"They are not dead, they are not dead!
Now that the sun, like a lion, licks his paws and goes
    slowly down the hill:
now that the moon, who remembers and only cares
that we should be lovely in the flesh, with bright, crescent feet,
pauses near the crest of the hill, climbing slowly, like a
    queen
looking down on a lion as he retreats.
Now the sea is the Argonauts' sea, and in the dawn
Odysseus calls the commands, as he steers past those
    foamy islands
wait, wait, don't bring the coffee yet, nor the *pain grillé*.
The dawn is not off the sea, and Odysseus' ships
    have not yet passed the islands, I must watch them still."

In Sandro Botticelli's The Birth of Venus, *the artist attempted to re-create the style of ancient Greek paintings; for instance, demure poses like Venus's were common in Greek art during the third and second centuries B.C.*

slain; and the flying horse Pegasus glides along. In addition to his *The Three Graces* and other mythological paintings, Rubens turned out 112 oil sketches illustrating the tales of Ovid's *Metamorphoses.*[85] About forty-five of these, including *The Apotheosis of Hercules*, still survive.

Particularly notable for his depictions of mythology was Nicolas Poussin, a seventeenth-century Frenchman who spent most of his career in Rome, where he was inspired by the works of Renaissance painters such as Botticelli. Some of Poussin's most important works include *The Triumph of Neptune, Venus Bringing Arms to Aeneas*, and *The Birth of Bacchus*. Morford and Lenardon write of him:

Like Rubens, [he] never ceased to draw inspiration from the classical legends. For him the world of classical mythology is an age of perfection, gone never to return. Among painters he is the most perfect interpreter of the classical myths, and those who wish to understand best what "classicism" means in Renaissance art should study the long series of drawings and paintings done by Poussin on mythological themes.[86]

Western musical composers, like writers and artists, have turned with great enthusiasm to the Greek and Roman myths. The earliest important music derived from these stories took the form of opera. One of the earliest operas on record, *Euridice*, created about 1600 by members of the Camerata, an artistic society based in Florence, Italy, was inspired by the Greek myth of Orpheus and Eurydice.[87]

As this new medium combining visual spectacle and complex, descriptive musical numbers rapidly became popular and spread across Europe, hundreds of composers turned out operas, many of them employing mythological settings. Among the most notable were *Giasone*, or *Jason* (1649), by the Italian Pier Francesco Cavalli, about the quest for the Golden Fleece; English composer Henry Purcell's work *Dido and Aeneas* (ca. 1689); *Orpheus and Eurydice* (1762) and *Iphigenia in Aulis* (1767) by Germany's Christoph Willibald Gluck; Frenchman Hector Berlioz's *The Trojans* (1856–1858), a masterful and majestic adaptation of Books Two and Four of Virgil's *Aeneid*; and in the twentieth century, *Oedipus Rex* (1927) by Russian composer Igor Stravinsky and *Troilus and Cressida* (1954) by Englishman William Walton.

Composers also adapted the myths to other musical forms. A well-known example is German Ludwig von Beethoven's ballet music titled *The Creatures of Prometheus* (1801) about the Titan who gave humans the gift of fire, a work scored for full orchestra. More exotic instrumental combinations were used by the twentieth-century English composer Benjamin Britten in his *Young Apollo* (1939), orchestrated for piano, string quartet, and string orchestra, and the lovely *Six Metamorphoses After Ovid*, styled for solo oboe.

One of the most popular modern musical forms, the American Broadway musical, has also borrowed material from classical mythology. Rodgers and Hart's *By Jupiter* (1942) is based on the story of Hercules' ninth labor, in which the legendary hero goes on a quest for the magical girdle of the queen of the Amazons.[88] In the course of the show, the Greek warriors use the power of love to conquer the famous warrior women. Other well-known examples are *The Golden Apple* (1953), a tuneful tragic-comic retelling of the Trojan War, and *The Gospel at Colonus* (1983), which creatively reenacts Sophocles' play *Oedipus at Colonus* in the setting of an American gospel service.

One of the most famous Broadway adaptations of mythology is Lerner and Loewe's *My Fair Lady* (1956). The musical (made into an Oscar-winning film in the 1960s) was based on English playwright George Bernard Shaw's 1913 play, *Pygmalion*, which updated the tale of Pygmalion and Galatea to London in Shaw's own time. Henry Higgins, an urbane phonetics instructor who, like his counterpart in the myth, at first disdains getting involved with women, transforms an uncultured street urchin, Eliza Doolittle, into a respectable lady. And in the process, of course, they fall in love. In a similar vein, echoes of Pyramis and Thisbe continue to resonate in Bernstein and Sondheim's equally famous *West Side Story*, which effectively transplants Shakespeare's tale of the tragic lovers Romeo and Juliet to the gang-infested streets of modern New York City.

Film Gives Mythology a New Visual Dimension

Because the medium of film combines elements of many other media, including writing, visual art, and music, from its inception shortly before the dawn of the twentieth century, film became a natural mode for retelling the classical myths. Most of the more than eighty existing films dealing directly with mythology were made in two cycles, the first lasting from the 1890s until about 1918, and the second from about 1953 to 1971. Among the silent films in the first cycle were the French *Ulysses and the Giant Polyphemus* (1905) and the American *In Cupid's Realm* (1908), *Neptune's Daughter* (1912), and *The Golden Fleece* (1918).

The first major cinematic retelling of the Trojan War was the Italian *The Fall of Troy* (1911). This film was an ambitious project for its time (the scene in which the Trojans pull the wooden horse into the city used six hundred extras), but its obvious use of miniatures and cardboard cutouts makes it seem crude in comparison to the 1956 Warner Brothers version, *Helen of Troy*, directed by Robert Wise. Al-

though the later film suffers from a rather tedious overemphasis of the love affair between Helen and Paris, it is appropriately spectacular in scope and often colorfully brings famous Homeric episodes to life. Noted film historian Jon Solomon reports:

The action scenes are terrific. . . . The thinly clad Greeks with their stout, round shields march on the mighty bastions of Troy under the cover of tall, wooden siege towers and huge battering ram. The Trojans desperately fight back with flaming arrows. The Greek attack suddenly bursts into flames and the spectacle of their long flight back to the ships is most memorable. . . . The film's most superior scenes are those which Homer more or less wrote: Achilles (Stanley Baker) grovels in the dirt as he grieves for the

A Confirmed Old Bachelor

The leading character Henry Higgins in George Bernard Shaw's Pygmalion *is as wary of women as was his counterpart, the sculptor Pygmalion, in the Greek myth. In this excerpt from Act II of the play, Higgins explains his reservations about women.*

"I find that the moment I let a woman make friends with me, she becomes jealous, exacting, suspicious, and a damned nuisance. I find that the moment I let myself make friends with a woman, I become selfish and tyrannical. Women upset everything. When you let them into your life, you find that the woman is driving at one thing and you're driving at another. . . . I suppose the woman wants to live her own life; and the man wants to live his; and each tries to drag the other on to the wrong track. One wants to go north and the other south; and the result is that both have to go east, though they both hate the east wind. . . . So here I am, a confirmed old bachelor, and likely to remain so."

dead Patroclus; Achilles quarrels bitterly with Agamemnon; Achilles drags Hector's (Harry Andrews) body in the dust; and Hector bids a touching farewell to his wife and infant child.[89]

Two other entries in the second cycle of mythological movies deserve special mention. The first is a 1955 Italian production, *Ulysses*, a credible and colorful version of Homer's *Odyssey*, starring Kirk Douglas in the title role. Though the English dubbing is often crude and the budget modest, the film authentically recreates most of the major episodes of the original work, including particularly effective renditions of the encounter with the Cyclops Polyphemus, the deadly songs of the sirens, Ulysses' conversations with the spirits of Achilles and other

dead heroes, and the climactic fight to the death with Penelope's suitors.

Even more effective overall was the American film *Jason and the Argonauts* (1963), loosely based on Apollonius's epic poem, the *Argonautica*. The film retains many of the original episodes, including King Pelias meeting the one-sandaled man (Jason, of course), and perhaps better than any other movie captures the titanic size, power, and haughty sense of superiority of the Greek gods. The real stars of the film, however, are the amazing special effects produced by Ray Harryhausen, the twentieth century's master of the stop-motion animation process.[90] His extraordinary skills breathe life into the grotesque harpies, bronze giant Talos, and other mythical monsters in one exciting and eye-popping sequence after another. Most

In this scene from the 1956 Warner Brothers film Helen of Troy, *Prince Paris (standing on chariot) attempts to beat back a group of attacking Greek warriors.*

Some Frustrated Modern Argonauts

Charles H. Schneer shot much of Jason and the Argonauts *in outdoor Mediterranean locations, which often proved expensive and difficult. In this excerpt from his book* From the Land Beyond Beyond, *film historian Jeff Rovin recalls one particularly frustrating incident.*

"As Schneer realized early in the planning stages of [the film], there was no way to shoot the adventure without a full-scale *Argo*. So he built one for $250,000 which . . . led to some rather remarkable shots as well as a near trauma for the producer. After losing time and money on several sunless days, with the crew idle and at full pay, Schneer finally had a clear day on which to do some shooting of the *Argo* at sea. Sailing into a Sicilian bay off 'the Isle of Bronze,' the producer coordinated the action and began filming. Suddenly, a Spanish galleon from the television series *Sir Francis Drake* came floating about the headland and spoiled an excellent [camera] set-up. Jumping from his command jeep on the beach, Schneer grabbed a megaphone and hollered, 'Get that out of here, you're in the *wrong century!*'"

effective of all is the climactic fight between Jason and the spawn of the dragon's teeth; Harryhausen portrays these earth-born warriors as relentlessly savage sword-wielding skeletons in what remains one of the greatest special-effects sequences ever filmed. Thanks to Harryhausen's wizardry, comments Solomon, "the film surpasses all others in recreating the fantastic aspects of Greek myth. . . . Through his genius, one's impression of the Greek mythological world is expanded into a new dimension of visual imagination."[91]

Thus, in leaping from the ancient manuscripts and onto printed pages, artists' canvases, musical scores, and movie screens, the Greek and Roman myths have been endlessly retold, translated, adapted, visualized, and memorialized; and thereby, gifted minds and hands have intricately interwoven them into the literary and artistic fabric of Western civilization. In this process, one still ongoing, these stories not only survived the extinction of the classical civilization that created them but also shaped and colored the cultures and worldviews of later Western societies, including our own. For this reason, they remain essential reading for every thoughtful person. As Max Herzberg puts it, "We are bound to the past in innumerable ways, and it is well to know the old myths in order that we may understand our own times."[92]

Notes

Introduction: Timeless Tales of Gods and Humans

1. Mark P. O. Morford and Robert J. Lenardon, *Classical Mythology*. New York: Longman, 1985, p. 3.
2. Edith Hamilton, *Mythology*. New York: New American Library, 1940, p. 16.
3. Peter Connolly, *The Legend of Odysseus*. New York: Oxford University Press, 1986, p. 78.

Chapter 1: Fire from Heaven: The Creation of the Gods and Humans

4. Hesiod, *Theogony*, in *Hesiod and Theognis*. Translated by Dorothea Wender. New York: Penguin Books, 1973, p. 26.
5. Hesiod, *Theogony*, in *Hesiod and Theognis*, p. 26.
6. Aristophanes, *Birds*, in Moses Hadas, ed., *The Complete Plays of Aristophanes*. New York: Bantam Books, 1962, p. 255.
7. Hamilton, *Mythology*, pp. 64–65.
8. Hesiod, *Theogony*, in *Hesiod and Theognis*, p. 39.
9. Delphi was the site where the famous oracle, a priestess (actually a succession of priestesses), supposedly acted as a medium between the gods and humans by delivering riddle-shrouded prophecies to pilgrims who asked questions. The ancient Greek traveler Pausanias visited Delphi about 180 A.D. and saw the object claimed to have been disgorged by Cronos. In his *Guide to Greece*, he described it as "a stone of no great size which the priests of Delphi anoint every day with oil."
10. Hesiod, *Theogony*, in *Hesiod and Theognis*, p. 45.
11. David Bellingham, *An Introduction to Greek Mythology*. Secaucus, NJ: Chartwell Books, 1989, pp. 32–34.

12. Homer's *Iliad* contains an alternate version of Aphrodite's origin, namely, that she was the daughter of Zeus and Dione, one of the minor deities known as Oceanids, or sea nymphs.
13. The Greeks feared and respected, but in general disliked, Ares, and he was not regularly worshiped in Greek cities, except in the northern region of Thrace, said to be his birthplace. By contrast, the more militaristic Romans admired their version of Ares—Mars—and honored him with temples and other tributes.
14. In some stories Hera bore Hephaestos alone, in retaliation for Zeus's creation of Athena on *his* own; other accounts claim Hephaestos was the son of both Zeus and Hera.
15. Max J. Herzberg, *Myths and Their Meanings*. Boston: Allyn and Bacon, n.d.g., pp. 13–14.
16. There was an element of truth in this belief, for Bronze Age Greece, dominated by the Minoans and Mycenaeans, was the source of most of the larger-than-life characters of the Greek myths.
17. W. H. D. Rouse, *Gods, Heroes and Men of Ancient Greece*. New York: New American Library, 1957, p. 19.
18. After many years, the hero Heracles (or Hercules), himself a descendant of Zeus, came upon poor Prometheus still chained to the rock. Heracles slew the eagle, released Prometheus from his predicament, and then persuaded Zeus to forgive the Titan and to welcome him back into the company of the gods.
19. This story shows that some of the Greek myths were strongly influenced by those of Middle Eastern peoples such as the Babylonians and Hebrews, whose own creation tales contained accounts of a great flood that only a handful of persons survived.

Chapter 2: Men Who Lived for Action and Glory: The Trojan War

20. C. M. Bowra, "Problems Concerned with Homer and the Epics," in C. G. Thomas, ed., *Homer's History: Mycenaean or Dark Age?* New York: Holt, Rinehart and Winston, 1970, p. 9.

21. Michael Grant, *The Rise of the Greeks*. New York: Macmillan, 1987, p. 147.

22. At least as early as the eighth century B.C., bards were reciting the *Iliad* and the *Odyssey*; the other epics in the Trojan cycle, apparently less esteemed literarily by ancient scholars than the first two, were probably composed a bit later. In the mid-sixth century B.C., or possibly earlier, professional epic reciters, called rhapsodes, including the Homeridae, or Descendants of Homer, began competing in public festivals, the winners of which may have received awards.

23. Apollodorus, *Bibliotheca*, in Rhoda A. Hendricks, trans., *Classical Gods and Heroes*. New York: Morrow Quill, 1974, p. 216.

24. Herzberg, *Myths and Their Meanings*, pp. 190–191.

25. Aeschylus, *Agamemnon*. Translated by Robert Fagles and excerpted in Bernard Knox, ed., *The Norton Book of Classical Literature*. New York: W. W. Norton, 1993, p. 308.

26. Homer, *Iliad*. Translated by W. H. D. Rouse. New York: New American Library, 1950, p. 20.

27. Homer, *Iliad*. Translated by E. V. Rieu. Baltimore: Penguin Books, 1950, pp. 288, 291.

28. Homer, *Iliad*, Rieu translation, p. 293.

29. Homer, *Iliad*, Rouse translation, p. 237.

30. Homer, *Iliad*. Translated by Richmond Lattimore. Chicago: University of Chicago Press, 1951, p. 444.

31. Virgil, *Aeneid*. Translated by Patric Dickinson. New York: New American Library, 1961, p. 28.

32. Virgil, *Aeneid*, Dickinson translation, pp. 36–37.

Chapter 3: Jason, Odysseus, and Aeneas: Three Journeys of Epic Adventure

33. Other ancient writers described episodes in Jason's life that took place after the recovery of the Golden Fleece. For instance, Euripides' great tragedy, *Medea*, deals with the grisly revenge exacted by the title character, who had helped Jason obtain the Fleece, after he rejects her for another woman.

34. Valerius Flaccus, *Argonautica*, in Rhoda A. Hendricks, trans., *Classical Gods and Heroes*, p. 183.

35. Charles Kingsley, *The Heroes*. Santa Rosa, CA: Classics Press, 1968, pp. 73–74.

36. The Greek word *harpyai* means "snatchers," and the Harpies were originally pictured (in Homer, for example) as snatching people's souls. Later, they earned a reputation for harassing people and fouling their food. In the *Aeneid* Virgil depicted them as birds with women's faces, an image that ancient artists frequently pictured.

37. This was the early Greek name for what we now know as the Black Sea. The later classical Greeks, having explored and colonized it, called it the Euxine, or Friendly Sea.

38. Apollonius, *Argonautica*. Translated by Peter Green and excerpted in Bernard Knox, ed., *The Norton Book of Classical Literature*, pp. 544–545.

39. Homer, *Odyssey*. Translated by E. V. Rieu. Baltimore: Penguin Books, 1961, p. 141.

40. Homer, *Odyssey*, Rieu translation, p. 142.

41. Homer, *Odyssey*. Translated by Robert Fitzgerald and excerpted in *The Norton Book of Classical Literature*, p. 138.

42. Homer, *Odyssey*, Rieu translation, p. 330.

43. Virgil, *Aeneid*, Dickinson translation, p. 58.

44. Virgil, *Aeneid*. Translated by Robert Fitzgerald and excerpted in *The Norton Book of Classical Literature*, pp. 661–662.

45. Dido's curse was Virgil's way of suggesting that the Punic Wars—the three bloody conflicts between Rome and Carthage that occurred two centuries before his time—along with Rome's ultimate victory over its rival, had been long fated to happen.

46. Virgil's contemporary, the historian Livy, provided a more detailed account of Romulus's exploits in his massive Roman history, thus helping to complete the Roman foundation myth. The first-century A.D. Greek writer Plutarch also wrote about Romulus and other important early Roman figures in his famous collection of biographies, *Parallel Lives* (or *Lives of the Noble Grecians and Romans*).

47. Virgil, *Aeneid*, Dickinson translation, pp. 141–142.

48. Augustus was Virgil's friend and patron and the poet's inclusion of the leader in Anchises' vision of Rome's future was calculated both as an homage to their friendship and as political propaganda to solidify Augustus's image as a great ruler fulfilling a divine destiny.

49. Virgil, *Aeneid*, Dickinson translation, p. 14.

Chapter 4: Triumphing over All Obstacles: Tales of Love and Lovers

50. Ovid, *Loves*, in *The Love Books of Ovid*. New York: The Book League of America, 1937, pp. 3–4.

51. Apuleius originally titled the work *Metamorphoses*, a conscious homage to Ovid's earlier work of the same name, which ostensibly retold myths involving miraculous transformations of one kind or another. Appropriately, Apuleius's work is about a youth who is transformed into a donkey and then back into a person. The title *The Golden Ass* was coined by the later Latin writer St. Augustine and be-

came so often repeated that eventually it largely replaced the original.

52. Apuleius, *The Golden Ass*. Translated by P. G. Walsh. New York: Oxford University Press, 1995, p. 76.

53. Apuleius, *The Golden Ass*, Walsh translation, p. 81.

54. Apuleius, *The Golden Ass*, Walsh translation, pp. 92–93.

55. Apuleius, *The Golden Ass*, in Rhoda A. Hendricks, trans., *Classical Gods and Heroes*, p. 287.

56. Ovid, *Metamorphoses*. Translated by Rolfe Humphries. Bloomington: Indiana University Press, 1967, p. 242.

57. Ovid, *Metamorphoses*, Humphries translation, p. 243.

58. Ovid, *Metamorphoses*, Humphries translation, p. 359.

59. Ovid, *Metamorphoses*, Humphries translation, p. 201.

60. Ovid, *Metamorphoses*, Humphries translation, p. 204.

61. Ovid, *Metamorphoses*, Humphries translation, p. 83.

62. Ovid, *Metamorphoses*, Humphries translation, p. 83.

Chapter 5: Cursed by the Gods: Divine Punishment for Human Folly

63. The main sources of the Tantalus legend are Homer's *Odyssey* and Pindar's *Odes*; the best source for Niobe's tale is Ovid's *Metamorphoses*; and the most complete ancient telling of the curse of the House of Atreus, including the fates of Agamemnon and his relatives, is Aeschylus's *Oresteia*, the trilogy of plays consisting of *Agamemnon*, *Libation Bearers*, and *Eumenides*.

64. The principal source for material about Oedipus is Sophocles' Theban play cycle, consisting of *Oedipus the King* (also known as *Oedi-*

pus Rex or *Oedipus Tyrannos*), *Antigone*, and *Oedipus at Colonus*. The main exception is the episode in which Oedipus meets the Sphinx, which Sophocles mentions only briefly; many ancient writers described this episode, including the first-century B.C. Greek historian Diodorus Siculus in his *Library of History*, quoted in this chapter.

65. Homer, *Odyssey*, Rieu translation, p. 187. Pindar gave an alternate version in which Tantalus was punished both for his pride and for stealing the divine ambrosia. His penalty was forever to hold a huge rock over his head and struggle to keep it from falling down and crushing him.

66. According to legend, Pelops journeyed from Asia Minor, his birthplace, to Greece, where he became the able ruler of the city of Elis; after his death, the large peninsula that makes up the southern third of Greece, in which Elis occupies a prominent position, became known as the Peloponnesus, or "Isle of Pelops," in his honor.

67. Ovid, *Metamorphoses*, in Rhoda A. Hendricks, trans., *Classical Gods and Heroes*, pp. 79–80.

68. Hamilton, *Mythology*, pp. 241–242.

69. Aeschylus, *Agamemnon*, in Richmond Lattimore, trans., *Aeschylus I: Oresteia*. New York: Washington Square Press, 1968, p. 89.

70. Aeschylus, *Libation Bearers*, in Richmond Lattimore, trans., *Aeschylus I: Oresteia*, pp. 143–144.

71. Diodorus Siculus, *Library of History*, in Rhoda A. Hendricks, trans., *Classical Gods and Heroes*, p. 108.

72. Sophocles, *Oedipus the King*, in Rhoda A. Hendricks, trans., *Classical Gods and Heroes*, pp. 113–114.

73. Sophocles, *Oedipus the King*. Translated by Bernard Knox. New York: Pocket Books, 1959, pp. 23, 25, 28–29.

74. Sophocles, *Oedipus the King*, Knox translation, pp. 56–57.

75. Sophocles, *Oedipus the King*, Hendricks translation, p. 152.

Chapter 6: Mining an Ancient Legacy: The Classical Myths in Popular Culture

76. In the fifth century B.C., the sophists, teachers who, for a price, dispensed "wisdom" about practical subjects, did much to undermine literal belief in the gods and traditional myths. There was a conservative social reaction to this trend, culminating in the trial of the philosopher Socrates in 399 B.C. for his supposed atheism. But in the following decades, intellectuals and educated people increasingly turned to the dictates of philosophy for guidance. Mythology suffered as a result; for example, Socrates' pupil Plato eliminated the Homeric legends from his ideal educational curriculum.

77. The same thing happened on an even larger scale during the first centuries B.C. and A.D., when eastern religions and cults spread to Rome, by this time master of the Mediterranean world. The Romans eagerly absorbed these foreign beliefs, either accepting them in place of the official religion, still presided over by the old Olympian gods, or simultaneously accepting the existence of both old and new gods as part of a larger universal truth.

78. Augustine, *The City of God*, 7.18. Translated by Marcus Dods in *Great Books of the Western World*, Vol. 18, *Augustine*. Chicago: Encyclopedia Britannica, 1952, p. 254.

79. From about the third century B.C. on, astrology was almost universally embraced in the classical world. Indeed, it became more like a religion than the science it was purported to be, as it tried to show how the heavenly bodies had a direct influence on human life. In this scenario the stars and planets were seen to have godlike powers, and therefore it seemed

only natural to assign them the names of traditional classical deities.

80. Morford and Lenardon, *Classical Mythology*, pp. 504–505.

81. Grant, *Myths of the Greeks and Romans*, pp. 330–331.

82. Act 1, scene 2, line 155; see any of the hundreds of versions in print.

83. Shakespeare used the tale of Pyramis and Thisbe more directly in *A Midsummer Night's Dream* in the scene in which a group of simple folk meet in the woods to rehearse their version of the old story.

84. Edgar Allan Poe, "To Helen," in Thomas Ollive Mabbott, ed., *The Collected Works of Edgar Allan Poe*, Vol. I, *Poems*. Cambridge, MA: Harvard University Press, 1969, pp. 165–166.

85. The sketches were part of a commission from King Philip IV of Madrid, who wanted Rubens to create full-sized paintings to adorn his royal hunting lodge. Very few of the larger works survive.

86. Morford and Lenardon, *Classical Mythology*, p. 518.

87. In the original tale, Orpheus was a musician whose playing was so beautiful it could calm wild beasts. When his beloved wife Eurydice died, he followed her into the underworld and played his lyre for Hades, who was so moved that he allowed her to leave and rejoin the living. The one condition was that Orpheus walk ahead of her and never look back until they had reached the earth's surface. At the last moment, he could no longer resist the temptation to look back, and when he did so, she was sucked back into the depths, never to return.

88. According to legend, Hercules (Heracles) married Megara, a Theban princess, and had children with her. Then in a fit of madness brought on by the goddess Hera, he killed his wife and children. Seeking purification, he journeyed to Delphi, where the oracle advised him to put himself in the service of King Eruystheus of Tiryns for twelve years. Eruystheus imposed upon Hercules twelve superhuman labors, among them killing a rampaging lion, capturing the fearsome Cretan bull, and acquiring the girdle of Hippolyta, queen of the Amazons.

89. Jon Solomon, *The Ancient World in the Cinema*. New York: A. S. Barnes and Company, 1978, p. 67.

90. The stop-motion process utilizes realistic-looking miniature models equipped with movable limbs, fingers, tails, and other appendages. The animator moves each of these parts a fraction of an inch, takes one frame of film, moves them again, takes another frame, and so on. When the film is projected at the standard speed of twenty-four frames per second, the illusion is achieved that the models are moving of their own accord. With the advent of computer-generated animation in the 1980s, hand-manipulated stop-motion films became less common.

91. Solomon, *The Ancient World in the Cinema*, p. 72.

92. Herzberg, *Myths and Their Meaning*, p. 4.

For Further Reading

David Bellingham, *An Introduction to Greek Mythology*. Secaucus, NJ: Chartwell Books, 1989. Explains the major Greek myths and legends and their importance to the ancient Greeks. Contains many beautiful photos and drawings.

Peter Connolly, *The Legend of Odysseus*. New York: Oxford University Press, 1986. An excellent, easy-to-read summary of the events of Homer's *Iliad* and *Odyssey*, including many informative sidebars about the way people lived in Mycenaean times. Also contains many stunning illustrations recreating the fortresses, homes, ships, and armor of the period.

Jane F. Gardner, *Roman Myths*. Austin: University of Texas Press, 1993. A finely written and mounted volume containing very readable versions of most of the important Roman myths and national tales.

Rhoda A. Hendricks, trans., *Classical Gods and Heroes*. New York: Morrow Quill, 1974. A collection of easy-to-read translations of famous Greek myths and tales, as told by ancient Greek and Roman writers, including Homer, Hesiod, Pindar, Apollodorus, Ovid, and Virgil.

Homer, *Iliad*. Retold by Barbara Leonie Picard. New York: Oxford University Press, 1960. And *Odyssey*. Retold by Barbara Leonie Picard. New York: Oxford University Press, 1952. Easy-to-follow, quick-moving introductions to Homer's classic works, which profoundly shaped Greek mythology and national character.

Charles Kingsley, *The Heroes*. Santa Rosa, CA: Classics Press, 1968. This is a reprint of the original book by Kingsley, the renowned nineteenth-century social reformer, university professor, and classical scholar, a work he wrote for his three children. Contains his superb retellings of the stories of Jason, Perseus, Theseus, and Heracles.

C. J. Naden, *Jason and the Golden Fleece*. Mahwah, NJ: Troll, 1980. A handsome retelling of the saga of the quest for the Fleece.

Don Nardo, *Ancient Greece; The Roman Republic; The Roman Empire*. San Diego: Lucent Books, 1994. These volumes present comprehensive general overviews of Greek and Roman civilization, providing a context to understand better the people for whose religion, arts, and everyday life classical myths were integral.

Don Nardo, *Greek and Roman Theater*. San Diego: Lucent Books, 1995; and Don Nardo, ed., *Readings on Sophocles*. San Diego: Greenhaven Press, 1997. These volumes provide valuable information about Sophocles, Aeschylus, and other

Greek playwrights whose works dramatized important mythological stories
and characters.

Don Nardo, ed., *Readings on Homer*. San
Diego: Greenhaven Press, 1998. This
useful volume contains several scholarly
yet readable essays about various aspects
of the *Iliad* and *Odyssey*, as well as about
Homer's style and impact, each essay by
a noted expert in the classics.

Ian Serraillier, *A Fall from the Sky: The Story
of Daedalus*. New York: Walck, 1966.
This version of the classic tale of
Daedalus and Icarus, who flew on
wings of wax, is geared specifically for
young readers.

Major Works Consulted

Aeschylus, *Oresteia*, in Richmond Lattimore, trans., *Aeschylus I: Oresteia*. New York: Washington Square Press, 1968. Aeschylus's famous trilogy, consisting of *Agamemnon*, *Libation Bearers*, and *Eumenides*, is one of the primary sources for the legends about the curse of the House of Atreus. Lattimore's translation is excellent. I have also used Paul Roche's commendable version, in *The Orestes Plays of Aeschylus*. New York: New American Library, 1962, which I recommend for the modern, realistic feel of its dialogue. A concise short summary of the Orestes plays appears in Edmund Fuller, *A Pageant of the Theater*. New York: Thomas Y. Crowell, 1965; and a very worthwhile longer synopsis in Michael Grant's *Myths of the Greeks and Romans* (see below).

Ernle Bradford, *Ulysses Found*. New York: Harcourt, Brace and World, 1963. A fascinating and meticulously researched exploration of the route Odysseus may have taken in his famous journey through the precivilized Mediterranean world.

Jan Bremmer, ed., *Interpretations of Greek Mythology*. Totowa, NJ: Barnes and Noble Books, 1986. A collection of essays by noted experts examining various aspects of ancient Greek mythology. Of interest mainly to scholars and mythology buffs.

Thomas Bulfinch, *Bulfinch's Mythology*. New York: Dell, 1959. This is one of several versions of this well-known and useful work, which is itself a modern compilation of two of Bulfinch's original books—*The Age of Fable* (1855), a retelling of the Greek and Roman myths, and *The Age of Chivalry* (1858), an account of the Arthurian legends.

Michael Grant, *Myths of the Greeks and Romans*. One of the twentieth century's most prolific and respected classical historians here delivers a fine rendition of the important Greek and Roman myths, along with plenty of background information and analysis.

Edith Hamilton, *Mythology*. New York: New American Library, 1940. Hamilton's excellent retelling of the Greek myths is still considered by many to be the best and most entertaining overview of its kind.

Max J. Herzberg, *Myths and Their Meanings*. Boston: Allyn and Bacon, n.d.g. A useful introduction to the major classical myths, formatted as a textbook with study questions, exercises, and reading lists.

Hesiod, *Theogony*, in *Hesiod and Theognis*. Translated by Dorothea Wender. New York: Penguin Books, 1973. In *Theogony*, the late-eighth-century B.C. Greek poet Hesiod presented the earliest known version of the creation of the world and the Greek gods. The work became an important cornerstone for the Greek and Roman myths in the following centuries.

Homer, *Iliad*. Translated by W. H. D. Rouse. New York: New American Library, 1950. Dr. Rouse's version of the first classic of Western literature is straightforward and easy to read. I have also consulted the sturdy translations by E. V. Rieu—Baltimore: Penguin Books, 1950—and Richmond Lattimore—Chicago: University of Chicago Press, 1951—as well as the more recent one by Michael Reck—New York: HarperCollins, 1994. For substantial synopses of the *Iliad* in English, I recommend Connolly's *The Legend of Odysseus*, Grant's *Myths of the Greeks and Romans*, Hamilton's *Mythology* (all three, see above), and Morford and Lenardon's *Classical Mythology* (see below). For Homer's *Odyssey*, I have relied mainly on E. V. Rieu's excellent translation—Baltimore: Penguin Books, 1961. Worthwhile summaries of the *Odyssey* appear in the four secondary sources just cited.

Mark P. O. Morford and Robert J. Lenardon, *Classical Mythology*. New York: Longman, 1985. This very well-written volume features fulsome background and analysis of the major Greek and Roman myths, as well as a section on the survival of those stories and characters in later literature, arts, music, and film. Highly recommended.

Ovid, *Metamorphoses*. Translated by Rolfe Humphries. Bloomington: Indiana University Press, 1967. A fine readable translation of the landmark telling of most of the important classical myths by the first-century B.C. poet Publius Ovidius Naso, popularly known as Ovid. Indispensable for any serious study of Greek and Roman mythology.

Stewart Perowne, *Roman Mythology*. London: Paul Hamlyn, 1969. This volume by Perowne—the noted historian, archaeologist, and author of several important works about Rome, including *The End of the Roman World*—is well written and nicely illustrated.

John Pinsent, *Greek Mythology*. New York: Peter Bedrick Books, 1986. A well-written synopsis of the subject, beautifully illustrated with numerous photographs, many in color, of relevant Greek locales, sculptures, vases, and so on.

H. J. Rose, *Religion in Greece and Rome*. New York: Harper and Brothers, 1959. This study by one of the acknowledged masters in the field remains one of the finest available overviews of Greek and Roman uses of myths, folklore, and religious rituals.

W. H. D. Rouse, *Gods, Heroes and Men of Ancient Greece*. New York: New American Library, 1957. An absolutely first rate retelling of the major Greek myths by a renowned classical scholar. (Dr. Rouse, who died in 1950, earned a prestigious reputation not only for his books but also for his twenty-six years of teaching Greek and Latin in Cambridge, England.) As noted above, I have also used Rouse's excellent translation of the *Iliad*.

Michael Wood, *In Search of the Trojan War*. New York: New American Library, 1985. An extremely well-written and entertaining examination of the myth of the Trojan War and how German archaeologist Heinrich Schliemann and other scholars proved that the legend was based on fact.

Additional Works Consulted

Apuleius, *The Golden Ass.* Translated by P. G. Walsh. New York: Oxford University Press, 1995.

Augustine, *The City of God.* Translated by Marcus Dods in *Great Books of the Western World*, Vol. 18, *Augustine.* Chicago: Encyclopedia Britannica, 1952.

David Bellingham, *An Introduction to Greek Mythology.* Secaucus, NJ: Chartwell Books, 1989.

C. M. Bowra, *The Greek Experience.* New York: New American Library, 1957.

———, *Homer.* New York: Charles Scribner's Sons, 1972.

Peter Connolly, *The Legend of Odysseus.* New York: Oxford University Press, 1986.

Will Durant, *The Life of Greece.* New York: Simon and Schuster, 1966.

Charles W. Eliot, ed., *Nine Greek Dramas by Aeschylus, Sophocles, Euripides and Aristophanes.* New York: P. F. Collier and Son, 1909.

Bernard Evslin, *The Adventures of Ulysses.* New York: Scholastic Book Services, 1969.

Jane F. Gardner, *Roman Myths.* Austin: University of Texas Press, 1993.

Charles M. Gayley, *The Classic Myths in English Literature and in Art.* New York: Ginn and Company, 1939.

Michael Grant, *The Classical Greeks.* New York: Charles Scribner's Sons, 1989.

———, *The Rise of the Greeks.* New York: Macmillan, 1987.

Jasper Griffin, *Homer: The Odyssey.* Cambridge, England: Cambridge University Press, 1987.

Moses Hadas, ed., *The Complete Plays of Aristophanes.* New York: Bantam Books, 1962.

G. M. Kirkwood, *A Short Guide to Classical Mythology.* New York: Holt, Rinehart and Winston, 1959.

Bernard Knox, ed., *The Norton Book of Classical Literature.* New York: W. W. Norton, 1993.

Richmond Lattimore, trans., *Greek Lyrics.* Chicago: Chicago University Press, 1960.

Pierre Léveque, *The Birth of Greece.* New York: Harry N. Abrams, 1994.

Peter Levi, *Atlas of the Greek World.* New York: Facts On File, 1984.

J. V. Luce, *Lost Atlantis: New Light on an Old Legend.* New York: McGraw-Hill, 1969.

Thomas Ollive Mabbott, ed., *The Collected Works of Edgar Allan Poe*, Vol. I, *Poems.* Cambridge, MA: Harvard University Press, 1969.

A. R. Hope Moncrieff, *Classic Myth and Legend.* New York: William H. Wise, 1934.

R. M. Ogilvie, *The Romans and Their Gods in the Age of Augustus.* New York: W. W. Norton, 1969.

Eugene O'Neill, *Mourning Becomes Electra*, in *Three Plays of Eugene O'Neill.* New York: Vintage Books, n.d.g.

Ovid, *Loves*, in *The Love Books of Ovid.* New York: The Book League of America, 1937.

Pausanias, *Guide to Greece* (in 2 volumes). Translated by Peter Levi. New York: Penguin Books, 1971.

Plutarch, *Lives of the Noble Grecians and Romans.* Translated by John Dryden. Chicago: Encyclopedia Britannica, 1952.

Betty Radice, *Who's Who in the Ancient World: A Handbook to the Survivors of the Greek and Roman Classics.* New York: Penguin Books, 1973.

Jane D. Reid, *The Oxford Guide to Classical Mythology in the Arts, 1300–1990s* (in 2 volumes). New York: Oxford University Press, 1993.

Jeff Roven, *From the Land Beyond Beyond: The Films of Willis O'Brien and Ray Harryhausen.* New York: Berkley Publishing, 1977.

Frances E. Sabin, *Classical Myths That Live Today.* New York: Silver Burdett, 1940.

George Bernard Shaw, *Pygmalion.* New York: Simon and Schuster, 1968.

M. S. Silk, *Homer: The Iliad.* Cambridge, England: Cambridge University Press, 1987.

Jon Solomon, *The Ancient World in the Cinema.* New York: A. S. Barnes and Company, 1978.

Sophocles, *Oedipus the King.* Translated by Bernard Knox. New York: Pocket Books, 1959.

C. G. Thomas, ed., *Homer's History: Mycenaean or Dark Age?* New York: Holt, Rinehart and Winston, 1970.

Virgil, *Aeneid.* Translated by Patric Dickinson. New York: New American Library, 1961.

Leonard Whibley, ed., *A Companion to Greek Studies.* New York: Hafner Publishing, 1963.

Index

Picture Credits

About the Author

Classical historian and award-winning writer Don Nardo has published more than eighty books. In addition to this volume on Greek and Roman mythology, his studies of the classical world include *The Roman Republic, Life in Ancient Rome, Life in Ancient Greece, The Age of Augustus, The Age of Pericles, Philip and Alexander: The Unification of Greece,* a biography of Julius Caesar, and others. Mr. Nardo also writes screenplays and teleplays and composes music. He lives with his wife, Christine, on Cape Cod, Massachusetts.